Carefree Gourmet Presents

Dazzling Desserts, Bountiful Brunch, Tea Anytime, Brazilian Bar-B-Que, Casual Cajun, and Classy Cocktail For up to 20 Guests

by

Andrea M. Olguin

Photographer: Pam Kietzman

AuthorHouse™
1663 Liberty Drive, Suite 200
Bloomington, IN 47403
www.authorhouse.com
Phone: 1-800-839-8640

AuthorHouse™ UK Ltd.
500 Avebury Boulevard
Central Milton Keynes, MK9 2BE
www.authorhouse.co.uk
Phone: 08001974150

First published by AuthorHouse 8/3/2006

ISBN: 1-4259-1661-9 (sc)

Printed in the United States of America
Bloomington, Indiana

This book is printed on acid-free paper.

Bloomington, IN

authorHOUSE

Milton Keynes, UK

Acknowledgments

We would like to thank all of our family and friends who supported us through tasting parties, recipe ideas, music suggestions, editing, and encouragements - you're the best!

Rod Olguin, Russell Gordon, Jackie Gordon, Ruth Kietzman, Robin Kietzman, Dr. Dale Kietzman, Dino and Cindy Putrino, Mike and Alice Sterling, Brad Smith & Barbara Koeing, Chris and Kelly Ryder, Kathleen Shannon, Michelle Rotherham and Kurt Cochran, Karen Balchunas, Lori Sandoval, Leora Lewis, Susie Sulzbach, Bill Welden, Celena Acala, Patrice and Eric Martin, Lola and Darrel Osborn, Liz Wojdak, Mary Jo Winder, Kimberly Glidden, and Bob Fowler (in kind memory)

Table of Contents

Greetings

Parties. Most of us love parties. We have fun attending them. We would even like to entertain on occasion. But the thought of entertaining may be so daunting that perhaps you haven't entertained in years or at all. Whether you work and can't squeeze in the time it takes to plan a party or you are shy about your talents and abilities, The Carefree Gourmet, the complete party planner, is for you. It includes everything from how to address the invitation to a schedule to keep you on track; the menu, recipes, even some relaxing ideas to help you enjoy your party too!   You can take it with you to the market, the bakery, the cleaners, anywhere you need to go so you don't forget something or have to rewrite lists.

This edition of The Carefree Gourmet is centered around six entertaining events that lend themselves to relaxing, splurging on yourself, focusing on the simple pleasures in life - delectable, mouth-watering temptations and the company of family and good friends. These parties can be held in the late morning, mid-afternoon, or evening. You can have an open house, entertain on a sunny porch, in the spring, outside with lots of flowers and family, or you can create an elegant evening by the fireplace, with champagne to sip as you nibble fresh strawberries dipped in whipped cream or warm melted dark chocolate.

These buffets are wonderful, in that many of the dishes can be prepared either weeks or days ahead of time, then frozen/defrosted or stored in airtight containers. Most items can be purchased from the neighborhood store. Set up and clean up are a breeze and these menu items make a wonderful presentation by themselves, so table decoration is a snap.

Buffets lend themselves to inviting more people than you could invite to a sit down party. It allows you to circulate amongst your guests freely and not spend so much time in the kitchen. So turn the page and start on your next party, no special occasion required; just having delightful friends is enough to celebrate!

Enjoy,
Andrea & Pam

P.S.   A few things you need to know about this book and the creators. This book was written by novice cooks. We don't claim to have gone to Le Cordon Bleu Chef School. We both have taken a few culinary courses, spent some time in a commercial kitchen, but for the most part, we simply enjoy cooking and entertaining. We both have regular full time jobs with husbands, kids, aging parents and siblings. Most importantly, we tested all of these recipes in a home kitchen with home tools, so we know they work! We hope you enjoy our creations. If so, look for announcements to additional Carefree Gourmet entertaining at www.CarefreeGourmet.com.

The Menus

The menu should be a flavorful mixture of colors and textures. Vibrancy in color, interest in texture, and wonderful aromas should entice your guests to sample many delicacies on your buffet. So that you don't spend too much time in the kitchen, the six menus include a mixture of homemade and freshly made purchased treats. If one of your guests has a delicious family recipe that they would like to share, you may choose to have them bring the prepared item. Just be sure you have the equipment to support the item (like a fondue pot for a dipping sauce), or ask your guest to provide all needed utensils. Variety is always a welcome addition to any buffet and may allow you to remove a similar item from your menu (one less to make or buy!). Also try to ensure the item isn't something that requires multiple utensils for serving, as your guests will be handling both their beverage and their plate.

The goal of any menu is to offer an array of choices, appealing to many and offering a variety of tastes and textures. Different levels of sweetness, richness and yes, calories for the figure conscience. If you have friends with special dietary requirements be sure to provide them something on the menu that meets their needs. Note: Be aware of food allergies, especially to items such as nuts. Don't grind nuts so finely that they are unrecognizable. It may help to identify dishes with a pretty note card.

These menus were planned with the intention of using the same kitchen utensils and serving pieces. And the recipes can be swapped between menus so that you may host another party of the same type but with a different variety of offerings. If you have a favorite recipe that is adored, by all means, add it to the menu, or substitute out a menu item. Just remember to add the ingredients to the shopping list and the "when to" to the time line. The grocery list is immediately following the recipes. Check your pantry for items you may already have and check them off your list if you don't need to purchase them. Some words of advice. Get into the habit of dating your spices and other baking ingredients once you open them, to take away the guessing game of knowing if the product is still good. Unless you cook and bake a great deal, buy in small quantities. One last bit of advice, baking is a science, be sure to measure accurately!

We hope these menu's inspire you to have a few friends over and enjoy their company!

Dazzling Desserts

- Sweet-Tart Lemon Bars (recipe)
- Strawberries with Powdered Sugar or Whipped Cream (purchase) or Chocolate Fondue (recipe)
- Cheesecake (can be purchased) with Raspberry Sauce (recipe)
- Brownies (purchase mix)
- Display Cake: fancy (bakery order/purchase)
- Zucchini Bread (recipe/make ahead and freeze)
- Chocolate Chip Pumpkin Bread (recipe/make ahead and freeze)
- Mousse Cake or Torte (purchase)
- Assorted Cheeses, Fruits, Crackers, and Nuts (purchase)
- Coffee
- Mulled Cider
- Tea
- Champagne Cocktails
- Johannesburg Riesling (or other sweet wine)
- Milk (child guests)

Bountiful Brunch

- Creamy Swiss Quiche (recipe)
- Broccoli Goat Cheese Quiche (recipe)
- Baked Hashbrowns (recipe)
- Fresh Fruit with Poppy Seed Dressing (recipe)
- Cinnamon Kahlua Coffee Cake (box mix adaptation)
- Blueberry Muffins (box mix)
- Cherry Claufutti (recipe)
- Croissants (purchase)
- Honey Baked Ham (purchase)
- Shrimp Cocktail (purchase)
- Coffee
- Tea
- Champagne and Mimosas
- Brunch Cocktail
- Orange, Pomegranate and/or Cranberry Juices

Tea Anytime

- Lemon Fruit Tart (recipe)
- Classic Cucumber Finger Sandwiches (recipe)
- Smoked Ham and Apricot Finger Sandwiches (recipe)
- Pesto Cream Cheese Finger Sandwiches (recipe)
- Smoked Salmon with Cream Cheese Sandwiches (recipe)
- Cranberry Orange Cream Scones (recipe or purchase from local tea house or bakery)
- Clotted Cream (recipe)
- Assorted Seedless Jams and Jellies; raspberry, blackberry (purchase)
- Fresh Strawberries and Raspberries - Spring/Summer or Pear and Apple Wedges - Fall/Winter (purchased)
- Fancy Chocolates (purchase)
- Fancy Cookies (purchase)
- Tea (Black Tea and Herbal)
- Iced Tea with A Splash (recipe)
- Champagne

Brazilian Bar-B-Que

- Chips and Guacamole, Sour Cream & Salsa (purchase)
- Marinated Chicken and Beef Kabobs - "Churrasco" (recipe)
- Marinated Shrimp Kabobs (recipe)
- Fiesta Rice - "Arroz" (recipe)
- Fresh Tomato Salad with Red Wine Vinaigrette (recipe)
- Black Bean Stew - "Feijoada Completa" (recipe)
- Coconut Cornbread (recipe)
- Little Cheese Custards - "Queijadinhas" (recipe)
- Baguettes (purchase)
- Flan - "Pudim" (recipe)
- Mango, Papaya, & Strawberry Margaritas (recipe)
- Assorted Beers
- Passion Fruit Iced Tea
- Lemonade
- Coffee

The Casual Cajun

- Jalapeno Popovers (purchase)
- Olive Tapenade (purchase)
- Assorted Breads (purchase)
- Assorted Sausages (purchase)
- Marinated Shrimp (recipe)
- "Grilled" Artichokes With Aioli Sauce (recipe)
- Dirty Rice (purchase)
- Mango Relish (recipe)
- Pound Cake with Fresh Fruit (purchase)
- Bread Pudding with Whisky Sauce (recipe)
- Bloody Mary's (recipe)
- Hurricanes (recipe)
- Assorted Beers
- Lemonade with Strawberries
- Soft Drinks
- Southern Pecan Coffee

The Classy Cocktail

- California Rolls (purchase)
- Shrimp Cocktail (purchase)
- Vegetable Platter (purchase)
- Hot Artichoke Dip (recipe)
- Asparagus Rolls (recipe)
- Spinach Balls (recipe)
- Crab Souffle with Assorted Crackers (recipe)
- Chocolate Fondue with Fruit and Pound Cake (recipe)
- Martinis (recipes)
- Assorted Beers
- Soft drinks
- French Roast Coffee

Getting Started

The next section is the planning of your party. How much money do you want to spend? What kind of party do you want to throw? What mix of friends and family do you want to invite? You will want to think through all these small but important details before the invitations go out. We hope you find this section helpful in reducing some of the stress of entertaining!

What Is Your Budget?

Your budget will determine the course of your party. It will determine the location, the type of party, the number of guests and the assortment of food and beverages you will serve. Nothing in this plan requires you to purchase expensive, speciality food items that may be also be difficult to find. Everything can be purchased at a regular grocery store, a quality bakery or at a unique grocer, like Trader Joes. You can trim costs as well by serving all nonalcoholic beverages. Or stick to a quality wine or champagne. Do not buy "jug" wine - it is tasteless and an insult to your guests. Also, be sure to purchase fruits and vegetables in season. Out of season items are always more expensive as they are usually grown is special hot houses or shipped from afar.

Borrow, borrow, borrow - serving pieces, dishes, coffee pots etc. Unless you are stocked with these kinds of apparatuses it will cost you a fortune to purchase it all for a party. If however, you plan on entertaining regularly, purchase as both money and storage space allow. If your family likes to entertain we suggest starting a co-op of serving pieces. Then share with each other. This reduces cost and storage needs.

Purchased goods, paper products (if you purchase quality plastic products, you can wash them and reuse them), rentals (try to borrow folding tables and chairs) and decorations can add up. Fresh flowers from a florist can add up too. Cut flowers from your garden or ask your neighbor for a few flowers from their garden. Fresh flowers from your garden will last longer than those from the florists. Farmer's markets are another great place to purchase fresh flowers at a reasonable price. Or purchase potted flowers from the local nursery or hardware store. Not only will this be less expensive, but you can also enjoy the plant for a longer period of time. If you are on a limited budget, but abundant on friends, do a potluck - have your friends bring a menu item. You can supply the menu ideas, recipes, location, eating utensils, beverages and a signature menu item.

Note: *It is always good to leave a little cash available for last minute purchases such as ice.*

The Guest List

After determining your budget and type of party you will need to start the guest list. For the most enjoyment, try to invite friends who know at least one guest, other than you, that have interests in common, or you think will hit it off. When you create your guest list, if you like, have a back up list in case folks happen to be busy on the day you have selected. That way, you can immediately send out more invitations, or if the party is very casual and you are good friends, you may call directly to extend an invitation. We have provided a guest list template for your use. We suggest you make copies so that you can reuse this template for all your parties.

Note: *If your guests don't know each other well, select some outgoing friends to "work the room" and visit with isolated guests.*

Party_____   Date_____

Y	N		Y	N	
☐	☐	_____	☐	☐	_____
☐	☐	_____	☐	☐	_____
☐	☐	_____	☐	☐	_____
☐	☐	_____	☐	☐	_____
☐	☐	_____	☐	☐	_____
☐	☐	_____	☐	☐	_____
☐	☐	_____	☐	☐	_____
☐	☐	_____	☐	☐	_____
☐	☐	_____	☐	☐	_____
☐	☐	_____	☐	☐	_____
☐	☐	_____	☐	☐	_____
☐	☐	_____	☐	☐	_____
☐	☐	_____	☐	☐	_____
☐	☐	_____	☐	☐	_____
☐	☐	_____	☐	☐	_____
☐	☐	_____	☐	☐	_____
☐	☐	_____	☐	☐	_____
☐	☐	_____	☐	☐	_____

The Invitation

Invitations set the tone of any party for the recipient. You can purchase invitations at your local party or stationary store. For those with Internet access you may also choose to send invitations via e-mail through such companies as bluemountain.com. Or for a quick get together with friends and family, forgo the formality and give folks a call!

If writing out your invitations, you can jazz them up with little effort. You can use a calligraphy pen (available at stationary, office supply and art stores) that have ink cartridges. If you are uncomfortable with this, use a quality pen and either handwrite or print (which ever is most legible) your invitations. Gold and silver pens are also available and add a nice, more formal touch to an invitation.

Be sure to include specifics in your invitation, for example, mention if it a christening or birthday party. Also add particulars like, "black tie", or "will be held outside", "no spiked heels, please." Be sure to include an RSVP with the phone number and if you like, best time to call.

Invitations should be carefully addressed for presentation, legibility and etiquette. Be sure to address the invitation properly in terms of ensuring correct titles. Below is an example of a properly addressed envelope. On page 10 you will find additional listings of salutations.

Sample Invitation Addressing

Mr. and Mrs. J. Smith
1423 North Rockwell Avenue
Los Angeles, CA. 91001

Mr. and Mrs. Jack Clark
1535 North Santa Rosa Avenue
Glendale, CA 91765

The Invitation Con't

Addressing invitations can be tricky, depending on living arrangements, marital status and the female preference of using or not using her spouses name. The following are examples of proper salutations:

Mr. and Mrs. Joe Smith (Standard Married)
Mrs. Joe Smith (Married Women)
Mr. Joe Smith (Single or Married Man)
Ms. Barbara Smith (Married Woman for whom you don't know the husbands first name or the woman prefers to be addressed by her first name)
Miss Nancy Smith (Young Woman)
Mr. and Mrs. Joe Smith and Family (Invitation is for entire family)
Mr. Joe Smith and Ms. Janet Johnson (Married Couple but Woman retained her maiden name)
Dr. Jane and Mr. Dan Johnson (Married Woman is a Doctor)
Ms. Barbara Smith (An unmarried couple living together are addressed on separate lines)
Mr. Jack Clark

Also, if you recently moved, or have invited new friends, enclose a map with directions to the location of your party. Be sure to include a directional sign NSEW to provide a sense of direction. If you have access to the Internet, you can obtain a map through a mapping service like MapQuest.com. Or, you can hand draw a map, but be sure to drive the route you show to verify that you haven't left out any important streets, or a turn you might take for granted etc.

Setting The Table & The Mood

The buffet table is your focal point. It should be both appealing and functionally laid out. Depending on the space available and the number of guests, you may choose to push the table against a wall so guests approach on one side or you can have it centered to offer all around access. Make sure to remove your dining room chairs from around the table and scatter them in other rooms for extra seating.

Your food should be at different levels (taller items in the back or center, depending on the location of your table). Your napkins, plates, and forks should be at the beginning of the table (both ends if table is centered) for easy access.

We would suggest that beverages be on a separate table if possible. This helps with guest traffic and congestion. Depending on the party, you will need room for the coffee pot (near an electrical outlet), the tea pot, the crock pot, a punch bowl, a champagne bucket, wine caddy, and all the accompaniments plus the cups, napkins and spoons. Don't use stirring sticks, they look tacky and don't work well. Also, have a basket for the empty sugar substitute packets and used spoons. Otherwise they will end up on the table creating a mess.

The table should look bountiful, so if your table is huge remove a leaf if possible. For most parties, use a neutral tablecloth (wild prints/patterns may detract from your food presentation), or a festive solid if it is a special holiday. Mix the colors and textures on the table top, for example, don't place all white items together. Make sure there is room for a few non-edible decorations such as candles or flowers.

Try to find solid platforms for your food. Use a coffee table, mantle or desk if necessary. Be careful of card-tables, as they can sometimes be wobbly when bumped by guests.

A Note About Music: Music adds to the environment of any party. Whether it's a classical piece or an energetic salsa, music helps set the mood of any event. Keep the music at a level which is conducive to conversation. If you have a CD player with multiple disk changer, and can set it at random; setting music to play for hours is a breeze. Just select appropriate CD's and let the player do the rest. If you don't have random, then you can still place in hours of music, it will be heard one album at a time. If you have a tape player, you can choose to create a selection on one tape, or use single tape and have a selection set out for replacement during the party. If you have a radio only, then select a music station that plays mostly music with little talking. A classical, jazz or new age station are good choices.

Note: *Take pictures, it is fun and you can share the photos with friends after they are developed.*

Decor, Ambiance & Music

For afternoon Tea or Dessert:
(A great garden party. Wonderful confections with lots of flowers and sunshine.)

Set up on a porch or patio. Invite families. Have outdoor seating on the grass. Use white chairs or put down blankets for children. Use quality disposable clear plastic dishes and eating utensils. Have lots of fresh flowers on the table, ones from the garden are best. If you don't have a nice selection of flowers, you can pick up small potted flowering plants from the gardening center at your local nursery or hardware store. Use doilies and white linens on the table. Have lots of ice for punch and iced tea.

The Tea Party is a great "ladies" party! Dress in floral prints. Wear gloves and a hat. Eat off of china (it doesn't have to match!). Drink from crystal glasses.   If you have extra hats or can get you hands on some boas, have them available for your guests to wear during the party. If this is an afternoon dessert party with male companions, add outdoor leisure games like bocce ball or croquette.

For evening Dessert:
(A great winter party. Sweets and lots of hot drinks.)

If you have a fireplace light it up (or turn it on!). This is a perfect evening party for the fireplace. In the fireplace, use fake logs that you can purchase at the store. They come in different burning times. This way you have a fire without needing to tend to it! Select classical or new age music to play softly in the background. Use glassware and china for a dressy event. You can use clear plastic if you don't have enough tableware. The table should be elaborate and abundant looking. Decorate with doilies, fresh flowers, and bunches of grapes. Have candles glowing around the house. Turn the lights down low. Use a white, cream or light colored linen table cloth to show off the food. If you have a glass table - leave the tablecloth off. Place desserts at different heights, in different shaped and textured vessels. This makes a great winter holiday party!

Note: *If you are hosting an outdoor party, don't forget to plan time in your schedule for gardening.*

For late morning Brunch:
(Perfect anytime you wish to enjoy a relaxing Sunday with friends.)

This can be semiformal or casual. You can sit inside or dine on the patio if weather permits. Use glassware and dishes if semiformal. Or you can use festive colored quality paper goods for a more casual event. Decorate with flowers without much scent so as to not distract from the aroma of your food or attract bugs if outdoors. (Also friends may have allergies). Winter brunches can be accentuated with plaids and warm, dark colors. Spring and summer parties should be accented with bright colors. Pick upbeat background music. This makes a great spring family gathering for the holidays, bridal or baby showers.

Brazilian BBQ
(This is a great casual party. Grilling with friends, playing outdoor sports like flag football, volleyball, horse shoes, you name it.)

The invitation to this party should spell out casual. This is a great party to partake in or watch sports. Use sturdy paper products for this party in bright colors (orange, yellow, green and turquoise).   Choose a bright striped pattern for your tablecloth that matches your paper products. This will really liven up the dark meat and beans. When the TV isn't on with the current game, select lively music - rock, classic and salsa. Hold this party indoors or out. This party doesn't need alot of fussy decor. Think simple and let the meal be the focul point. This makes a great guys party - Father's Day or birthday.

For the Casual Cajun
(This is the BEST night party! Light the house with dozens of candles and turn off all the lights, not unlike a bar in New Orlean's .)

Decorate the table with a black tablecloth, mardi gras beads, masks and other metallic decorations. Metallic colors that are especially good are gold, silver, green, purple and fuchsia. You can use colored paper produts or plates that match your color theme. Play Louisiana Jazz and blues. This makes a great Halloween or birthday party.   **Important Note:** Don't have a "candlelight" party if you are inviting children or others who would find it difficult to move about with limited lighting.

For Evening Cocktails
(This is a HOT party in more ways than one!)

This party requires that the oven be on for a long period of tme. So host this prty on a cool evening in Spring, Fall or Winter! Have your guests dress up! Be classy! High heels for the ladies and suits for the gents! Serve on glass, crystal or china. Get out the silver! Polish it! Make those glasses sparkle! Use cloth napkins if you have them. If not, use a quality printed napkin. Use neutrals for the main colors to accent your crystal and sliver. Cream, white and black with an accent of red is nice. Make your guests feel like they are at a 1940's cocktail party. Put on Ella Fitzgerald, Nat King Cole, etc. Light candles. Put up twinkle lights (Christmas tree lights) outside in your trees.

Note: *Some cities have noise ordinances. Be aware of the volume of the music, especially after 10:00 pm.*

Essential Tools & Supplies

- ❏ Electric hand or stand mixer
- ❏ Food processor
- ❏ Measuring spoons
- ❏ Dry measuring cups
- ❏ Liquid measuring cups
- ❏ Spatula
- ❏ Wooden spoons
- ❏ Slotted spoon
- ❏ Pastry brush
- ❏ Sifter
- ❏ Bowls for mixing (sm, med & lrg)
- ❏ Bread loaf pan
- ❏ Bundt pan
- ❏ Cookie sheet
- ❏ Pie dish (2)
- ❏ 9x13x2 bake pan
- ❏ 8 x 8 baking dish
- ❏ Casserole dishes (3)
- ❏ Muffin pan (12 muffins)
- ❏ Knives (serrated, chopping, paring)
- ❏ Hand-held strainer
- ❏ Double broiler

- ❏ 1 1/2 qt sauce pan
- ❏ Oven mitt/pot holders (2)
- ❏ Steamer/colander for steaming
- ❏ Small frying pan
- ❏ Medium frying pan
- ❏ 6-8 qt stock pot
- ❏ Blender
- ❏ Wine & beer bottle opener
- ❏ Can opener
- ❏ Shot glass
- ❏ Cheese grater
- ❏ Wooden or metal skewers
- ❏ Martini shaker
- ❏ Cooling rack
- ❏ Coffee maker (minimum 10 cup)
- ❏ Plastic storage containers
- ❏ Foil
- ❏ Plastic wrap
- ❏ Wax paper
- ❏ Paper towels
- ❏ Trash bags
- ❏ Ziplock baggies - 1 gallon size
- ❏ Cutting board

The Measurements

The following symbols will be utilized in the recipes.

c Cup

T Tablespoon

tsp Teaspoon

oz Ounces

lb Pound

qt Quart

pkg Package

Conversions:

1 stick butter = 1/2 cup (8 T)

1 T = 3 tsp

2 T = 1 fluid oz

4 T = 1/4 c or 2 fluid oz

1/3 c = 5 1/3 T

1/2 c = 8 T

1 c = 16 T

1 pint liquid = 16 fluid oz or 2 c

1 quart = 2 pints or 4 c

Essential Serving Pieces

Although we have specified the serving pieces required for each food and beverage item on the menu or recipe, we have compiled one list to assure that you have gathered all the proper tools prior to the day you need them. Use this list when calling friends or family to borrow. Write their names down next to the borrowed item, that way you will know to whom to return it to after the party.

- ❏ Thermal coffee carafe
- ❏ Tea kettle
- ❏ Tea pot
- ❏ 15 coffee cups or mugs
- ❏ 15 champagne & wine glasses
- ❏ 15 martini glasses
- ❏ 20 tall drinking glasses
- ❏ 40 napkins
- ❏ 30 forks & spoons
- ❏ Cake server (2)
- ❏ Gravy boat or small pitcher
- ❏ 25 - 30 dessert & salad plates
- ❏ 20 dinner plates
- ❏ 2 tablecloths
- ❏ Pretty dish cloths (2)
- ❏ Oval platter (3)
- ❏ Round platter (5)

- ❏ Rectangular platter: large
- ❏ Crystal or glass bowl; large
- ❏ Crystal or glass bowl; small (6)
- ❏ Wide shallow bowl
- ❏ Baskets lined with linen napkins (2)
- ❏ Pitcher (3)
- ❏ Sugar bowl & creamer
- ❏ Pedestal bowl (2)
- ❏ Honey jar or bowl
- ❏ Fondue pot with long forks
- ❏ Raised cake plate
- ❏ Flat basket (2)
- ❏ Basket: large
- ❏ Large bucket or ice chest for beer, soda etc.
- ❏ Champagne or Ice bucket
- ❏ Serving knife & spoon
- ❏ **Optional:** Silver tea set

NOTES

The Recipes

The recipes are grouped by party type. But remember, after you have tried the parties, feel free to mix and match to create you own menus. You will need to create your own shopping lists, but you can easily do that by finding the items on the lists we have provided. You can do the same for creating your own timelines. Use the recipes to bring potluck items to someone else's party. Again, they are great for that since many of the items can be prepared ahead of time. Good luck and happy food preparation. Remember to have a good time while cooking. It is especially fun when you are cooking with a good friend or someone you love!

From top center, Fresh Strawberries with Powdered Sugar and Chocolate Fondue; Cheese and Fruit Platter; Chocolate Torte, Lemon Bars, Brownies and Cheesecake with Raspberry Sauce.

The Dessert Buffet

Delicious, decadent - this is not a party for dieters! So tell your friends to eat light the week before so they can indulge! Fresh ingredients are a must for successful cooking and baking and is **very** important for this party's success. If you have baking soda, baking powder, or spices, that have been around since ancient times, dump them! Their shelf life is only 6 months once they are opened. If you use a baking powder that is old, your cake/bread/muffin, won't rise properly and you will be disappointed and your dessert ruined. The cost of your ruined dessert more than out weighs the cost of a new baking powder. Here's to successful baking! Good Luck!

What You Need For This Party:

Serving Pieces:

1 large crystal or glass bowl

2 small crystal or glass bowls

1 fondue pot with long forks

3 round platters (if you have a raised cake plate substitute it for 1 platter)

3 oval platters

2 flat baskets lined with pretty napkins

1 small gravy boat or pitcher

1 crock pot or large sauce pan

1 sugar bowl & creamer

1 shot glass

1 champagne or ice bucket & a pretty towel

20 small plates

20 forks

15 spoons

20 coffee cups

20 tall glasses (for iced coffee)

15 wine & champagne glasses each

20+ napkins

Cooking Utensils:

large mixing bowl

medium mixing bowl

1 1/2 qrt. sauce pan

double boiler (substitute 2 qrt sauce pan)
8x8 glass baking dish

9x13 glass baking dish

2 bread loaf baking pans

baking sheet

electric mixer

blender

mesh strainer

knives (serrated, chef and paring)

wooden spoon & rubber spatula

sifter

measuring spoons, cups and glass measurer

coffee pot

wine opener

Notes

Fresh Strawberries with Chocolate Fondue.

Strawberries with Powdered Sugar or Whipped Cream or Chocolate Fondue

Number of Servings 20

Serving Dishes   Large crystal or glass bowl, fondue pan with forks, small crystal or glass bowl

Preparation Time   20 minutes

Cooking Time   10 minutes

Can You Double   Yes

Can You Freeze   Yes, up to 6 months (chocolate sauce only)

4 pints of fresh strawberries,
1 (1 lb) box powdered sugar
1 pint (2 c) heavy cream
10 oz best-quality bittersweet or semisweet chocolate, like Lindt, cut into small pieces

Clean and hull strawberries; place in a bowl. Decide what you will be serving with your strawberries; powdered sugar, whipped cream and/or chocolate fondue. Pour powdered sugar into a small, decorative bowl. Scoop whipped topping, such as Cool Whip into a decorate bowl. Refrigerate until ready to serve. Melt chocolate in a double boiler or in a sauce pan over low heat. Stir continually to avoid burning. Once melted, remove from heat. Pour cream into a 1 1/2 quart saucepan set over medium heat. When the cream begins to simmer, lower the heat and add the melted chocolate. Whisk for 1 minute over low heat, then turn off the heat. Continue whisking until the mixture is smooth. Cool slightly before using. The sauce will remain liquid at room temperature for about 2 hours, then it will thicken. You can soften it by reheating it on low over the stove top and whisking until heated through.

Note: Because strawberries are seasonal, you may substitute bananas, pineapple or kiwi. Be sure to add the fruit to your grocery list.

Fancy Display Cake

Number of Servings	15
Serving Dishes	Elevated Cake Plate
Preparation Time	None
Cooking Time	None
Can You Double	Yes, if you buy two
Can You Freeze	Depends on the filling (ask your baker)

Search out the most terrific bakery or patisserie for your fancy cake. You want to display something marvelous, that would be just too time consuming for you to bake. Select something with multiple layers, and an interesting filling. Something that looks beautiful-fancy. Don't plan on buying ahead of time and freezing. Order and pick up the day of the party. Only look into freezing if you have leftovers and don't want to eat them right away.

Cheesecake with Raspberry Sauce

Number of Servings	12
Serving Dishes	Cake plate, small pitcher
Preparation Time	20 minutes
Cooking Time	30 minutes
Can You Double	No, make two separate recipes
Can You Freeze	Yes, up to three months

3 oz of white chocolate, broken into 1 inch pieces
2 (8 oz) packages of cream cheese, at room temperature
1/3 c of sugar
2 tsp of vanilla
2 large eggs
1 chocolate crumb pie crust (available in the baking aisle of the supermarket)
Fresh strawberries or raspberries for garnish

Preheat oven to 350 degrees with the rack in the center position. In a double broiler, or a small bowl set over (not in) a pan of simmering water, melt the chocolate. Stir gently with a rubber spatula until smooth. In a food processor or 1 1/2-quart mixing bowl, using an electric mixer set on low, process or mix the cream cheese together with the sugar, vanilla, and eggs. When well mixed, add the chocolate and continue mixing or processing until just blended (do not over mix). Pour and scrape the mixture into the chocolate crumb crust and bake for 30 minutes, or until the outer edge is very light golden brown and slightly bubbled and a small damp spot remains in the center. Cool at room temperature for 1 hour, then refrigerate for at least 4 hours or overnight. Garnish with berries (strawberries halved and placed cut side down.)

Note: *If short on time, buy a frozen, premade cheesecake from your local store. Defrost according to package and garnish with fruit. Still make the raspberry sauce. If you choose to purchase, you will need to remove the cheesecake ingredients from the shopping list.*

Raspberry Sauce

Offer this as a wonderful accompaniment to the cheesecake.

2 (10 oz) packages of frozen raspberries, slightly defrosted and liquid reserved
1 (8 oz) container of best quality seedless raspberry jam
1/4 c raspberry liquor, like Chambord (optional but adds great flavor!)

Combine raspberries, jam and liquor in a food processor or blender and puree until smooth. Set a wide mesh strainer over a bowl and pour puree into the strainer. Using a rubber spatula or back of a wooden spoon, press the puree through the sieve, leaving the seeds behind. Cover and refrigerate until ready to serve. Pour into a gravy boat and place next to the cheesecake.

Zucchini Bread

Number of Servings	2 loaves (24 servings)
Serving Dishes	Basket lined with linens
Preparation Time	20 minutes
Cooking Time	50 minutes
Can You Double	No, make two batches
Can You Freeze	Yes, wrap in foil, put in a freezer bag.

If you have a garden, like we do, making zucchini bread from your harvest is fun! Sometimes the zucchini gets away from us and is HUGE. Not to fret! Cut up the zucchini in small pieces, remove the large seeds. If you have a food processor, this is the time to use it! You will have grated zucchini in a jiffy. However, if you need to use a hand grater, just give yourself some time to rest, or do a small batch at a time. This bread is easy to make, and freezes beautifully. If you are adding nuts, we suggest the hazel or pecan. Walnuts can sometimes overpower the subtle flavor of the zucchini. Be sure to toast the nuts on a cookie sheet at 300 degrees for 10 minutes for the best flavor.

3 c flour	1 c oil
1 tsp salt	2 c sugar
1 tsp baking soda	3 eggs
1/4 tsp baking powder	3 tsp vanilla
1T cinnamon	2 c grated zucchini
1/2 tsp allspice	1 c chopped nuts, hazel, pecan or walnut (optional)

Preheat oven to 325 degrees. Mix the dry ingredients together. In a separate bowl, beat together the oil and sugar. Add eggs, vanilla and zucchini one at a time to the oil/sugar mixture. Mix flour and oil mixture together. Fold in nuts. Bake for 50 - 60 minutes. Cool in pans. Turn out on a rack. If you are going to freeze, wrap in foil and then in plastic wrap or a freezer bag. Thaw, unwrap, slice and platter for your party.

Chocolately Brownies

Brownies

Number of Servings	24
Serving Dishes	Oval platter
Preparation Time	15 minutes
Cooking Time	30 minutes
Can You Double	No, make two separate batches
Can You Freeze	Yes, wrapped airtight up to 2 months

Here we recommend choosing either of the following boxed brownie mixes: Ghirardelli Double Chocolate Brownie Mix (very chocolaty, fudgy with a hardcrust top) or Betty Crocker Original Supreme brownie mix with syrup pouch, family size (chocolaty, cake-like texture). Make according to package directions. Ingredients may vary slightly. Read ingredients list and adjust grocery list accordingly. Some people like nuts in their brownies. You can jazz up a box mix by adding your favorite chopped nuts. Toast nuts at 300 degrees for 10 minutes on a cookie sheet for the best flavor. We suggest making one batch with nuts and one without!

eggs
oil
water
2 boxes of brownie mix
1 c chopped nuts (walnuts or pecans) - optional

When ready to serve, cut brownies into square and arrange on your platter. Cover with plastic wrap to keep the brownies from getting dried out on the edges. Remove plastic wrap just prior to guests arrival.

Chocolate Chip Pumpkin Bread

Number of Servings	16
Serving Dishes	Basket lined with a pretty napkin
Preparation Time	20
Cooking Time	20 - 25 minutes for muffins, 50 minutes for loaves
Can You Double	No, make two batches
Can You Freeze	Yes, wrap in foil, seal in freezer bag

1/2 c sliced, unblanched almonds
1 2/3 c all-purpose flour
1 c granulated sugar
1 tsp baking soda
1/4 tsp baking powder
1/4 tsp salt
1 tsp cinnamon
1/2 tsp nutmeg

1/2 tsp ginger
1/2 tsp allspice
2 large eggs
1 cup plain pumpkin (half of a 1 lb can)
1/2 c (1 stick) butter, melted
1 c (6 oz) chocolate chips
nonstick cooking spray

Preheat oven to 350 degrees. Put almonds on a baking sheet or pie pan and bake about 5 minutes, just until lightly browned; watch carefully so the almonds don't burn. Slide almonds off of the cookie sheet so they cool quickly (can place on a cutting board or wax paper, plate etc.) Grease two bread loaf pans with cooking spray. Thoroughly mix the dry ingredients together in a large bowl. Whisk eggs, pumpkin and butter until well blended. Stir in almonds and chocolate chips. Pour over dry ingredients and fold in until dry ingredients are moistened. Fill loaf pans 2/3 full and bake 50 minutes. Test by pressing on bread, if it springs back, it is done. Turn out on rack to cool. Wrap in a plastic bag and keep for up to 2 days. Reheat before serving. Slice and place in a lined flat basket.

Mousse Cake or Chocolate Torte

Number of Servings	12
Serving Dishes	Platter or Cake Plate
Preparation Time	None
Cooking Time	None
Can You Double	Yes, Order or Purchase 2
Can You Freeze	Ask Bakery or Read Package (for leftover's only)

Purchase this from a local bakery or grocery store. Do a test purchase ahead of time and taste the cake, or get a recommendation from a friend, if possible to find one you especially like. For example, in the Los Angeles area, Trader Joes carries a wonderful chocolate torte in the freezer section. It looks great, is easily decorated and virtually takes no time to prepare - just remove it from the freezer and let it thaw!

Assorted Cheeses, Fruits, Crackers and Nuts

Number of Servings	12
Serving Dishes	Platter and basket
Preparation Time	15 minutes
Cooking Time	None
Can You Double	Yes, double the quantity purchased
Can You Freeze	No

Purchase this from specialty grocery store or deli. Pick a nice assortment of cheeses. Think about your guests and what they would like. Do they like mild cheeses or more flavorful selections. If you aren't sure, offer a small mix of both. Here are some suggestions: Swiss, cheddar, havarti, jack (basics); goat cheese, stilton, brie, (more variety). Select a nice assortment of crackers that don't crumble easily. Fruits that go well with cheese include apples, pears, and grapes. Adding sprinkles of whole fresh strawberries and/or raspberries adds nice color. Nuts also go well with cheese and the salt is appealing to some folks for whom the desserts may have "sweetened out."

The time spent on this item is all on presentation. See the photo for a suggestion on how to lay out this platter. This is when you can be creative. Set the cheese out one hour before your guests arrive. The cheese will taste better and will be easier to cut and spread.

Sweet-Tart Lemon Bars

Sweet-Tart Lemon Bars

Number of Servings	24 bars
Serving Dishes	9x13 in pan to bake, an oval platter to serve
Preparation Time	20 minutes
Cooking Time	45 minutes
Can You Double	Yes (use two separate pans)
Can You Freeze	Yes (cut and wrap in wax paper then place in a freezer bag)

2 sticks (8 oz unsalted butter, softened)
2 1/4 c unbleached all-purpose flour, measured after sifting
1/4 c plus 1/3 c confectioner's sugar
4 large eggs
2 c granulated sugar
8 T freshly squeezed lemon juice
1/2 tsp baking powder
grated rind of 1 lemon

Preheat oven to 350 degrees with the rack in the center position. Spray a 13 x 9 inch pan with vegetable spray (quick and easier than spreading butter)

Place butter, 2 cups of flour, and 1/4 cup of the confectioner's sugar in a food processor or the bowl of an electric mixer and process or mix until the dough forms a ball. Press the dough into the bottom of the prepared pan, forming a 1/2 inch rim around the edges. Bake for 15 minutes.

Using a food processor, mixer or whisk, mix together the eggs, granulated sugar, lemon juice, remaining 1/4 cup of flour, the baking powder, and lemon rind until smooth. Pour the mixture over the center of the cooked dough, and spread it to the edges.

Return the pan to the oven and bake for another 30 minutes, or until the filling has set and the edges are golden. Cool completely at room temperature. Sift the 1/3 cup of confectioner's sugar over the top and cut into bars and place on oval platter.

The Dessert Buffet Beverages

How to Brew a Great Cup of Coffee Try to borrow a large coffee urn to make approximately 20 cups. This will ease the need for making coffee (average drip maker is 8 cups) every 30-45 minutes. Or you can use a coffee thermos to always keep two pots going. The coffee in the thermos will actually stay fresher as it won't continue to cook on the burner. Use quality, fresh, regular flavored coffee (i.e. Colombian) from whole beans. If you don't have a grinder, have the beans ground where you purchased the coffee (a few days before, sealed in an air tight container). Use the proper grind for the type of coffee maker you are using. Use two tablespoons of ground coffee per 8 ounce cup of cold water (either tap water or bottled if your city's water isn't palatable). We would recommend using de-caffeinated coffee, this way all your guests can enjoy the coffee, otherwise, you will need to make two separate pots which is cumbersome. Don't forget to serve half & half creamer, sugar and a sugar substitute with your coffee setup.

Coffee Liqueurs To offer a little variety to your coffee-drinking guests, we suggest coffee liqueurs. When serving coffee with liquors, fill the coffee mug two-thirds full. Add 1/2 jigger or 2 tablespoons per mug. Top with real whip cream (can be made or purchased in the can), do not use non-dairy topping. Recommendations for liqueurs are Bailey's Irish Cream, Kahlua and Blackberry brandy. There are many others to choose from. However, don't go gung ho as a little goes a long way, unless your guests are coffee-aholics, you will be storing this for years if you purchase too much.

Iced coffee (the afternoon garden party) brew coffee as you would normally (i.e. 40 spoonfuls for a 20 cup coffee maker). Let the brew cool to room temperature, pour into a glass pitcher and then add lots of ice.

Mulled Cider This is fun in the fall and winter. It makes the house smell great too. You can heat this in a large sauce pan, but a crock pot is best. You can purchase mulling spices from the grocer or other specialty grocery stores. Follow directions and heating guidelines. Garnish with cinnamon stick for a nice touch.

Tea Not everyone enjoys coffee. Tea is a nice alternative. Be sure to offer a few different varieties. Standards like orange pekoe; English breakfast and Earl Grey are always a good bet. Also include one or two of decaf blends. We suggest serving tea with milk, honey, sugar cubes and lemon wedges.

Wine: Dessert wines are best with sweets. Try a Sauterne, Riesling or Gewurztraminer. Or you can go with a red, like a Madeira, a port, or a Syrah port. They go well with chocolate.

Champagne If you have a champagne bucket, now is a great time to use it. Place some crushed ice and a little water into the bucket and place the champagne in the bucket with a towel wrapped around it to soak up the condensation.

The Grocery List - Dessert Buffet

Two weeks before the party

- ☐ Vegetable Spray
- ☐ 1 lb Unsalted Butter
- ☐ 1 5 lb bag Unbleached Flour
- ☐ 1 Box Powdered (Confectioner's) Sugar
- ☐ 1 5 lb bag Granulated Sugar
- ☐ 1/2 dozen Extra Large Eggs
- ☐ 1 c Heavy Cream (Whipping)
- ☐ 1-10 oz Semisweet Chocolate
- ☐ 1-8 oz White Chocolate
- ☐ 2-8 oz Cream Cheese
- ☐ 1 Chocolate Crumb Pie Crust
- ☐ 2-10 oz Package of Frozen Raspberries
- ☐ 1-16 oz Hershey Chocolate Syrup
- ☐ 1 c Pecans
- ☐ 1 c Walnuts
- ☐ 1 c Dates
- ☐ 1 pint Whole Milk
- ☐ 1 sm Vegetable Oil
- ☐ 1 c Honey
- ☐ 1 can (6 oz) Roasted Almonds
- ☐ 1 c Semisweet Chocolate Chips
- ☐ 1 qt Orange Juice
- ☐ 1 12 oz can Pumpkin
- ☐ 4 Zucchini
- ☐ 1 Seedless Raspberry Jam
- ☐ 1 pkg Cinnamon Sticks
- ☐ 2 liters Apple Cider
- ☐ 4 bottles of Champagne
- ☐ 4 bottles of Wine
- ☐ 1 pkg Loose tea
- ☐ Baking Powder
- ☐ Cloves, ground
- ☐ Cinnamon, ground
- ☐ Baking Soda
- ☐ Allspice
- ☐ Nutmeg

- ☐ Mulling spices
- ☐ Salt
- ☐ Vanilla
- ☐ 1 pint Raspberry Liqueur (optional)
- ☐ 1 pint Coffee Liqueurs (Baileys Irish Cream/ Kahlua/Vandermindt) (optional)
- ☐ Candles
- ☐ Matches
- ☐ Sterno/Fuel (for fondue pot)

Two days before party

- ☐ 1 qt Cream
- ☐ 4 Lemons
- ☐ 1 lb Coffee Beans
- ☐ 1 qt 1% Milk (optional)
- ☐ 1 pt flavored cream (optional)
- ☐ 1 pt Whipping Cream
- ☐ Assorted cheeses - Cheddar, Havarti, Brie, Jack, Smoked Gouda

Day of party

- ☐ 8 pint baskets of Strawberries
- ☐ 2 pint baskets of Raspberries
- ☐ 1 bunch each, red and green grapes
- ☐ 4 Kiwi
- ☐ 2 Apples
- ☐ 2 Pears
- ☐ 1 pt Whipping Cream
- ☐ Grapes for the table
- ☐ Flowers or Small Flowering Plants
- ☐ Garnish: 2 bunches of Leafy Green Lettuce, 1 bunch of Daisies, 1 large bunch of Mint

The Time Line - Dessert Buffet

Four weeks before the party
- ❏ Determine Budget
- ❏ Identify Location
- ❏ Determine Date/Time/Ambiance
- ❏ Compile Guest List
- ❏ Buy more invitations if necessary
- ❏ Address and Mail Invitations (Especially at holiday time, it is important to mail your invitations early because friends get booked)

Two weeks before party
- ❏ Make pumpkin and zucchini bread (wrap tight in plastic wrap and foil, then freeze)
- ❏ Assess party set up needs: linens/serving pieces/dinnerware etc.
- ❏ Table Cloth   ❏Napkins   ❏Forks   ❏Spoons   ❏Small Plates   ❏Coffee Cups
- ❏ Champagne Glasses   ❏Wine Glasses   ❏Cups for Children
- ❏ Place rental order if needed (chairs/dinnerware) **Earlier if a holiday party**
- ❏ Main grocery shopping (see shopping list)

Note: *Pick out your outfit before the party. If it needs to be cleaned or pressed, take it to the dry cleaners.*

One week before party
- ❏ Pick up dinnerware (plastic/borrowed)
- ❏ Pick up borrowed serving platters (glass/metal/ceramic)
- ❏ Make Chocolate Dipping Sauce, store in airtight container in refrigerator

Two days before party
- ❏ Make raspberry sauce and refrigerate
- ❏ Bake brownies (cover tightly, do not cut)
- ❏ Pick up dry cleaning (of linens or outfit if needed)
- ❏ Confirm rental order if placed

One day before party
- ❏ Bake cheesecake (refrigerate). If purchased and frozen, thaw in refrigerator
- ❏ Bake lemon bars (cover tightly, do not cut)
- ❏ Defrost breads
- ❏ Set table with linens and decor (not perishables), set out serving pieces and utensils

The Time Line Continued - Dessert Buffet

Day of party (4 hours before guests arrive)
- ❒ Purchase last minute groceries
- ❒ Pick up baked goods
- ❒ Pick up/have delivered rentals
- ❒ Arrange flowers
- ❒ Prepare coffee maker with ground coffee and water; but don't start yet
- ❒ Cut and platter lemon bars and brownies (cover tightly)

Day of party (30 minutes before guests arrive)
- ❒ Put beaters in freezer to chill (for 20 minutes)
- ❒ Put cider in crock pot w/mulling spices
- ❒ Reheat chocolate dipping sauce in a double broiler (a pan sitting over another pan filled with water). If you don't have one, put chocolate in a regular sauce pan over low heat and stir continuously until completelyheated through. Watch that bottom does not scorch. Pour into fondue pan.
- ❒ Place desserts and cheeses on table
- ❒ Turn on coffee maker
- ❒ Whip whipping cream until stiff peaks appear, place in bowl and refrigerate. If this is too much hassle, purchase Cool Whip and place in a pretty bowl. Purchase 2-3 cartons - don't forget to add to your grocery list!

Note: *1 1/2 hours before the party, stop, bathe, relax, rest, listen to soothing music, eat a lite meal and dress.*

From top center, Chilled Champagne and Orange Juice, Shrimp Cocktail, Blueberry Muffins, Broccoli and Goat Cheese Quiche, Creamy Swiss Quiche, Croisants with Raspberry and Apricot Jam, Cherry Claufutti, Cinnamon Kahlua Coffee Cake, Fresh Fruit, Baked Hashbrowns, and Honey Baked Ham.

The Brunch Buffet

Sunday brunch is a wonderful way to enjoy friends or family. Breakfast, which is usually a rushed event during the week, can be leisurely enjoyed. Cereal is replaced by hot dishes and freshly baked goods. You can enjoy a few cups of coffee or better yet, a sparkling glass of champagne. This is the time to splurge on breakfast to be enjoyed inside or out. We've created a palette that will appeal to both those seeking familiar a homestyle breakfast and those seeking a little flare. So invite a few friends or the family over for a relaxing Sunday morning and have a mimosa on us!

What You Need For This Party

Serving Pieces:

2 pedestal or medium glass or crystal bowls
2 small glass or crystal bowls
3 round platters
1 large oval or round platter
1 flat basket lined with a pretty napkin
1 small pitcher or gravy boat
3 casserole or glass pie dishes
1 casserole dish
1 butter dish or small plate
1 serving knife and fork
1 creamer and sugar bowl
1 shot glass
1 champagne or ice bucket & a pretty towel
2-3 pitchers (for juices & cocktail)
20 small plates
20 forks
15 spoons
20 coffee cups
20 tall glasses (for juice)
15 champagne glasses
20+ napkins

Cooking Utensils:

large mixing bowl
medium mixing bowl
small mixing bowl
1 1/2 qt. sauce pan
medium frying pan
bundt cake pan
9x13 inch glass baking dish
muffin pan
electric mixer
blender
knives (serrated, chef and paring)
wooden spoon & rubber spatula
whisk
measuring spoons, cups and glass measurer
cheese grater
can opener
coffee maker and thermos

Creamy Swiss Quiche.

Creamy Swiss Quiche

Number of Servings	8
Serving Dishes	Casserole
Preparation Time	15
Cooking Time	30 -35
Can You Double	Yes
Can You Freeze	No

1 c milk
3/4 c half & half
8 oz Swiss cheese
4 eggs, lightly beaten
8 slices of bacon
1 t salt
1/4 t pepper
1 t chives, chopped finely
1/8 t nutmeg
9-inch deep dish pie crust (in the frozen section)

Preheat oven to 450 degrees. Cook the bacon until crisp. Drain on a paper towel. Bake the frozen pie crust for five minutes. Remove pie crust from oven and reduce oven temperature to 400 degrees. In a bowl, mix the milk, cream cheese, eggs, crumbled bacon, salt, pepper, chives, and nutmeg. Carefully pour the mixture into the prepared pie crust. Cover with aluminum foil to protect the pie crust from burning. Bake for 30 to 35 minutes or until a knife inserted comes out clean. Transfer to a rack and cool for 15 minutes. Cut into 8 wedges.

*If you are serving more than 12 guests you will need to make three quiches. We suggest you make a second Creamy Swiss Quiche.

Broccoli and Goat Cheese Quiche.

Broccoli and Goat Cheese Quiche

Number of Servings	8
Serving Dishes	Pie dish or plate
Preparation Time	15
Cooking Time	30 -35
Can You Double	Yes
Can You Freeze	No

1 c small broccoli florets
3 eggs
2 green onions, thinly sliced
1 1/2 c milk
1/4 t salt
1/4 t pepper
1 t chives
1/8 t nutmeg
6 oz goat cheese
9-inch deep dish pie crust or a pastry sheet (in the frozen section)

Preheat oven to 425 degrees. Bake pie crust for 8 minutes. Remove from oven, reduce oven temperature to 350 degrees. In a medium saucepan, bring lightly salted water to boil. Add broccoli and cook until able to pierce with a fork, but still crispy. Drain well and dry on paper towels. In a bowl, lightly beat eggs. Add green onions, milk, salt, pepper, and nutmeg. Scatter the broccoli and drop small clumps of goat cheese evenly in the pie crust. Pour the egg mixture into the pie crust. Bake for 35 to 40 minutes or until a knife inserted comes out clean. Transfer to a rack to cool for 15 minutes. Cut into 8 wedges.

Note: We took the pie crust out of the aluminum pie tin and put it in our own casserole dish. You can do this too! If the crust breaks apart, just mush all back into a bowl and re-roll it out. Doesn't fit perfect? That's OK, look at ours, it looks like it has wings. We used the pastry sheet; if you do too, don't prebake the pastry sheet like you would if you used pie crust or it will burn!

Cherry Claufutti

Cherry Claufutti

Number of Servings	12
Serving Dishes	10 in round deep dish pie pan or shallow casserole dish
Preparation Time	15 minutes
Cooking Time	45 minutes
Can You Double	No
Can You Freeze	No

A claufutti is a simple custard-like French country dessert. The mixture for a claufutti resembles a thick pancake or crepe batter. This recipe is really easy and the batter can be made quickly. For this brunch, we used cherries. Peaches or apricots are other favorite fruits that could be used. Using canned fruit is convenient and tastes perfectly acceptable. Just be sure to garnish your finished dish with fresh fruit.

4 large eggs
¾ c sugar
1 c milk
1 T cognac or rum
2 tsp vanilla
¾ c all-purpose flour
Pinch of salt
1 lb sweet cherries (frozen cherries, thawed and patted dry, or canned cherries, drained and dried, can be used) Other fruits can be used in this same method.

Preheat the oven to 375 degrees. Butter a 10-inch diameter, deep dish pie pan (or a shallow casserole dish will do).

Beat the eggs and sugar until frothy, about 2 minutes (this can be done in a blender). Add the milk, cognac and vanilla and beat until smooth. Stir in the flour and a pinch of salt. Distribute the cherries (or other fruit) over the bottom of the pie or tart pan.

Pour the batter over the cherries and place the pie pan on a baking sheet. Bake the claufutti for 10 minutes; reduce the oven temperature to 350 degrees and bake until the top has puffed (it will sink on cooling) and a toothpick inserted in the center comes out clean, about 35 minutes more. Transfer to a rack and cool for about 20 minutes.   Dust with powdered sugar if desired and/or fresh fruit as a garnish.

Cinnamon Kahlua Coffee Cake, Blueberry Muffins, and Croissants.

Cinnamon Kahlua Coffee Cake

Number of Servings	12
Serving Dishes	Platter
Preparation Time	15 minutes
Cooking Time	55 - 60 (for bundt cake pan)
Can You Double	No (this recipe already is)
Can You Freeze	No

2 boxes of Pillsbury Cinnamon Swirl quick bread/coffee cake (or similar product)
4 eggs
1 c water
1/2 c Kahlua
1/2 c sour cream

Preheat oven to 350 degrees. Grease and flour (don't skip this step or the cake will stick and pull apart) bottom of a bundt cake pan.

Combine quick bread mix, eggs, water, kahlua and sour cream in a large bowl. Beat with a spoon or mixer until smooth. Pour half of the batter into the bundt pan. Sprinkle all of the swirl mix (cinnamon and sugar mixture). Pour the remaining batter over the swirl mix; spread carefully to cover. Bake approximately 55 - 60 minutes or until the loaf springs back when gently poked with a finger. While cake is baking, make the glaze. Note: if you don't have a bundt pan, use a loaf pan for each bread. Adjust baking time according to box mix.

Glaze
3/4 c powdered sugar
2 T softened butter
1 T Kahlua

Beat until smooth. Spoon over lukewarm cake. It will melt slightly. You will have leftover glaze.

Cool cake in pan on cooling rack, 15 minutes. Loosen edges with a knife or metal spatula; remove from pan. Serve warm or cool. Store leftovers tightly wrapped.

If you are going to use loaf pans, you do not need to make a second batch of the glaze, you will have enough if you use the recipe provided. Let the loaf cool slightly in the pan, then turn over onto the serving platter. Spoon glaze over the lukewarm loaf, let cool completely and then slice.

Baked Hashbrowns

Number of Servings	12
Serving Dishes	9 x 13 baking dish
Preparation Time	15 minutes
Cooking Time	1 hour, or until bubbly and lightly browned
Can You Double	Yes, if you have a large pan, if not, make two batches.
Can You Freeze	No

1 c thinly sliced green onions
1 c (4 oz) shredded, reduced fat extra sharp cheddar cheese
2 T butter, melted
1/4 tsp pepper
1/4 tsp salt
32 oz of frozen hash browns, thawed
16 oz fat-free sour cream
1 can (10 oz) of reduced-fat, condensed cream of mushroom soup
cooking spray
1/2 tsp paprika

Preheat oven to 350 degrees. Make sure you have thawed the hash browns (at least two hours out). When ready, combine the onions, cheddar cheese, butter, pepper, hash browns, sour cream, and mushroom soup in a large bowl. Spray a 9 x 13 baking dish with cooking spray. Spoon in hashbrown mixture, spreading evenly. Sprinkle with paprika. Bake for one hour, or until bubbly and lightly browned.

Honey Baked Ham

Number of Servings	24
Serving Dishes	Large platter
Preparation Time	5 minutes
Cooking Time	20
Can You Double	Yes
Can You Freeze	Yes

10 lb Honey Baked Ham

Preheat oven to 350 degrees. The ham is already cooked. It just needs to be heated. Place ham (wrapped in foil packaging) in a large casserole and bake for 20 minutes until heated through. Also place the serving dish (if oven safe) in the oven to heat. Remove foil from ham and place on warmed serving platter. The ham is already sliced for easy serving. Note: Honey baked hams are more expensive than those you can purchase at the local grocers, but they are delicious and easy to serve. If you don't have a local store, you can order via a catalogue or website at www.honeybaked.com If this is not convenient, go ahead and order a bone in ham from you local grocer's butcher. You will have to slice it before plattering.

Blueberry Muffins/Croissants

Number of Servings	24
Serving Dishes	Basket
Preparation Time	10 minutes
Cooking Time	20
Can You Double	Yes
Can You Freeze	No

This is a quick muffin recipe. Its all out of a box!

Duncan Hines Bakery Style Blueberry muffin mix is the best. Can't find it? Select the box mix that looks as good as possible (look for crumb toppings). Make the muffins according to the package directions.

Purchase one dozen freshly baked croissants. If you can't find any at a bakery, you can use the ones in the refrigerator section of the grocery store and bake according to directions. Warm up the croissants in the oven, wrapped in foil for 15 minutes prior to serving. Arrange in basket with the blueberry muffins. Serve with butter that has been set out to room temperature (no one likes squishing their baked goods with hard, cold butter!)

Shrimp Cocktail.

Shrimp Cocktail

Number of Servings	20
Serving Dishes	Pedestal and small glass bowl
Preparation Time	5 minutes
Cooking Time	None, 20 minutes to defrost
Can You Double	Yes
Can You Freeze	No

4 bags of frozen, tail on, shelled cooked shrimp
2 jars of Trader Joes or Heinz regular or zesty cocktail sauce
1 lemon (for garnish)

Defrost frozen shrimp according to package directions. By no means leave the shrimp out on the counter to defrost. Shrimp spoils very easily. If you forget to defrost in the refrigerator, you can quickly defrost by emptying the shrimp into a strainer and running the shrimp under cold water for 5 minutes. We arranged our shrimp in a pedestal bowl with the cocktail sauce on the side in a small glass bowl. Make sure you fill whatever bowl you use with crushed ice first to keep the shrimp cold. Again, it will spoil at room temperature. Cut lemons in wedges or slices, whichever looks best with your bowl.

Fresh Fruit with Poppy Seed Dressing

Number of Servings	20
Serving Dishes	Platter or pedestal bowl and small pitcher
Preparation Time	45 minutes
Cooking Time	None
Can You Double	Yes
Can You Freeze	No

To make the poppy seed dressing:

1 c honey	1 c vegetable oil
1 /4 tsp salt	1 T grated onion
1/2 c vinegar	1 1/4 tsp dry mustard or prepared mustard
	2 tsp poppy seeds

For the dressing, combine all ingredients in a quart jar. Shake to mix. Refrigerate. Shake again before serving. Cut up fresh fruits such as watermelon, cantaloupe and honeydew (remove rind), kiwi, nectarines, and strawberries (summer) or grapefruit, oranges, apples and avocados (winter). Arrange on a platter or in a pedestal bowl and sprinkle with raspberries and blueberries. Let guests spoon dressing over fruit.

Champagne, Orange Juice and Mimosas.

The Brunch Beverages

Mimosas This takes only about 5 minutes and should **not** be made ahead of time or the Champagne will go flat. Make a batch as needed. Mix two quarts of freshly squeezed, chilled orange juice (or best quality concentrate) and 1 bottle of chilled champagne in a large pitcher. Each batch will make 8 to 10 servings.

Champagne Cocktails This requires a nice champagne or sparkling wine, select a dry variety for best taste. You will need Angostura or other bitters and sugar cubes. Place a sugar cube in a champagne or wine glass, add 2-3 drop of the bitters onto the sugar cube. You can do this up to one hour before serving. When ready to serve, fill the glass with chilled champagne. Each bottle of champagne will provide 5 to 6 servings depending on the size of your glass. A fluted champagne glass is recommended.

How to Brew a Great Cup of Coffee Try to borrow a large coffee urn to make approximately 20 cups. This will ease the need for making coffee (average drip maker is 8 cups) every 30-45 minutes. Or you can use a coffee thermos to always keep two pots going. The coffee in the thermos will actually stay fresher as it won't continue to cook on the burner. Use quality, fresh, regular flavored coffee (i.e. Colombian) from whole beans. If you don't have a grinder, have the beans ground where you purchased the coffee (a few days before, sealed in an air tight container). Use the proper grind for the type of coffee maker you are using. Use one teaspoon of ground coffee per 8 ounce cup of cold water (either tap water or bottled if your city's water isn't palatable). We would recommend using de-caffeinated coffee, this way all your guests can enjoy the coffee, otherwise, you will need to make two separate pots which is cumbersome. Don't forget to serve half & half creamer, sugar and a sugar substitute with your coffee setup.

Coffee Liqueurs To offer a little variety to your coffee-drinking guests, we suggest coffee liqueurs. When serving coffee with liquors, fill the coffee mug two-thirds full. Add 1/2 jigger or 2 tablespoons per mug. Top with real whip cream (can be made or purchased in the can), do not use non-dairy topping. Recommendations for liqueurs are Bailey's Irish Cream, Kahlua and Blackberry brandy. There are many others to choose from. However, don't go gung ho as a little goes a long way, unless your guests are coffee-aholics, you will be storing this for years if you purchase too much.

Juices You will want to have a large pitcher of orange juice for the Mimosas and simply to drink. We also think offering other varieties is both interesting and provides more options for those who choose not to drink alcoholic beverages and don't care for a hot drink. We suggest cranberry and pomegranate, one tart and one sweet. They are both beautiful in color and offer a variety of taste. Juices pre-made, either freshly squeezed (best tasting but can be full of pulp) or from concentrate in the refrigerator section of your grocer are more convenient but also can be more expensive. Orange and cranberry juices can be found in the frozen section in concentrate form. Pomegranate must be purchased from the cold aisle.

The Time Line - Brunch Buffet

Two weeks before the party

- ☐ 1 c butter
- ☐ 32 oz frozen hashbrowns, country style or regular
- ☐ 3 9-inch deep dish frozen pie crusts
- ☐ 5 cans of frozen orange juice
- ☐ 5 bottles of Champagne 750 ml
- ☐ 1 sm bottle of Kahlua
- ☐ 2 boxes of Duncan Hines blueberry muffin mix
- ☐ 1 box (2 if making bundt cake) Pillsbury Cinnamon Swirl cake mix
- ☐ Sugar or sm box of sugar cubes
- ☐ 1 box powdered sugar
- ☐ 8 oz honey
- ☐ Nutmeg
- ☐ 1 sm jar poppy seeds
- ☐ Pepper
- ☐ Salt
- ☐ 1 sm dry or prepared mustard
- ☐ Vinegar
- ☐ Vegetable oil
- ☐ Nonstick vegetable cooking spray
- ☐ 10 oz lite cream of mushroom soup
- ☐ 1 10 oz jar spicy or regular cocktail sauce
- ☐ 24 decorative paper or clear plastic plates
- ☐ 48 lunch size decorative napkins
- ☐ 1 pkg each, clear plastic forks, knives, & spoons
- ☐ 24 clear plastic champagne glasses

One day before the party

- ☐ 6 oz goat cheese
- ☐ 4 oz shredded lowfat extra sharp cheese
- ☐ 16 oz Swiss cheese
- ☐ 16 oz lite sour cream
- ☐ 6 oz regular sour cream
- ☐ 3 1/2 c milk
- ☐ 16 oz half & half
- ☐ 13 eggs
- ☐ 16 slices of bacon
- ☐ 3 pkgs Canadian bacon
- ☐ 1 bunch of chives
- ☐ 2 bunches green onions
- ☐ 1 small bunch of broccoli
- ☐ 1 onion
- ☐ Quality coffee beans, ground if you don't have a grinder
- ☐ 3 bags of frozen shrimp, cooked and deveined

- ☐ **Summer Fruits**
- ☐ 1/4 watermelon
- ☐ 1 cantaloupe
- ☐ 1 honeydew melon
- ☐ 4 kiwi
- ☐ 4 nectarines
- ☐ 2 baskets of strawberries

- ☐ **Winter Fruits**
- ☐ 4 grapefruits
- ☐ 5 oranges
- ☐ 2 avocados
- ☐ 2 apples

Day of the party

- ☐ 1 dozen croissants from bakery, or purchase refrigerator dough

The Grocery List - Brunch Buffet

Four weeks before the party
- ❑ Determine budget
- ❑ Identify location
- ❑ Determine date/time/ambiance
- ❑ Compile guest list
- ❑ Purchase invitations
- ❑ Address and mail invitations (Especially at holiday time, it is important to mail your invitations early because friends get booked)

Two weeks before party
- ❑ Assess party set up needs: linens/serving pieces/dinnerware etc.
- ❑ Place rental order if needed (chairs/dinner ware)
- ❑ Main grocery shopping (see shopping list)
- ❑ Pick up dinnerware (plastic/borrowed)

Two Days before party
- ❑ Make poppy seed dressing and refrigerate
- ❑ Pick up dry cleaning
- ❑ Confirm rental order if placed

One Day before party
- ❑ Bake coffee cake, let cool, then wrap tightly in plastic wrap
- ❑ Make orange juice and put in refrigerator (if you don't have freshly squeezed)
- ❑ Bake blueberry muffins, let cool, store in air-tight container
- ❑ Set table with linens and decor (not perishables), set out serving pieces and utensils
- ❑ Refrigerate Champagne
- ❑ Make final run to the grocery store

Day of party (3 hours before guests arrive)
- ❑ Prepare quiche to stopping point-see recipes
- ❑ Pick up croissants or bake refrigerator dough
- ❑ Pick up/have delivered rentals
- ❑ Prepare coffee for brewing
- ❑ Cut fruit, platter and wrap tightly with platstic wrap
- ❑ Arrange flowers
- ❑ Slice coffee cake, platter and wrap in plastic
- ❑ Assemble hashbrown dish

Day of Party (1 hour before guests arrive)
- ❑ Assemble the quiches and bake
- ❑ Bake hashbrowns
- ❑ Prepare beverage accompaniments

Day of Party (15 minutes before guests arrive)
- ❑ Wrap baked goods in foil and warm
- ❑ Brew coffee
- ❑ Warm Canadian bacon
- ❑ Set out beverage accompaniments

Day of Party (when guests have arrived)
- ❑ Remove hot dishes from warm oven, set on table
- ❑ Place fruit and dressing on table
- ❑ Make and serve beverages

Note: *1 1/2 hours before the party, stop, shower, put on music, and dress.*

NOTES

NOTES

From Top Left: Iced Tea With A Splash, Fresh Fruit Platter, Smoked Salmon and Cream Cheese Finger Sandwiches, Smoked Ham and Apricot Finger Sandwiches, Pesto and Cream Cheese Finger Sandwiches, Cucumber Finger Sandwiches, and Cranberry Orange Cream Scones with Clotted Cream and Jam.

The Tea Buffet

Tea is an old fashioned past time. It is quite popular today as a special gathering with friends; a time to dress up, meet with your girlfriends or mom and sisters and enjoy a truly feminine pastime. So don your flowered dress, hat and gloves and bring this celebration home. All of the recipes are quick to complete and the menu can be substituted with purchased items if you feel pressed for time. For example, you could order the scones from a local bakery or tea shop and order the fruit tart from a local bakery or restaurant. The key to planning ahead on this party is to clean all of your serving pieces ahead of time. Select a pretty dress and invite the girls over for a leisurely afternoon!

What You Need For This Party:

Serving Pieces:
1   medium flat glass bowl or platter
4   small glass or crystal bowls
2   round platters (if you have a raised cake
     plate substitute it for 1 platter)
3   oval or round platters
1   flat basket lined with a pretty napkin
1   large pitcher
1   creamer and sugar bowl
1   champagne or ice bucket & a pretty towel
20 small plates
20 forks
15 spoons
20 tea cups & saucers
20 tall glasses (for iced tea)
15 champagne glasses

Cooking Utensils:
large mixing bowl
medium mixing bowl
small mixing bowl
cookie sheet
sifter
cutting board
electric mixer
colander
knives (serrated, chef and paring)
fork, rubber spatula, wooden spoon
measuring spoons, cups and glass measurer
cheese grater
tea kettle and serving tea pot
small glass bowl

Cranberry Orange Cream Scones with Clotted Cream and Jam.

Cranberry Orange Cream Scones

Number of Servings	12
Serving Dishes	Platter or basket lined with linen napkin
Preparation Time	20 minutes
Cooking Time	15 - 17 minutes
Can You Double	Yes, make in two rounds and cut each into 12 pieces
Can You Freeze	Yes, store in airtight container, up to two months. Defrost covered.

2 c all-purpose flour
1 T baking powder
3/4 tsp salt
1/4 c plus 2 T sugar
3/4 c dried cranberries (you will find them with the raisins; Oceanspray is one brand you can find in the grocery store. If you can't find them, use currants)
Finely grated peel of one large orange (about 2 tsp)
1/4 c orange juice
1 c heavy cream
3 T unsalted butter, melted

Preheat oven to 425 degrees. Put oven rack in center position. Use an ungreased cookie sheet. Don't use a dark one as they have a tendency to burn the bottom of your baked goods. Sift flour, baking powder, salt and 1/4 c of sugar together in a medium size mixing bowl. Mix with a fork to combine. Add orange peel and cranberries and mix. Then add orange juice and cream and mix with a fork until the mixture holds together. The mixture will be sticky.

Lightly spread flour on a wood cutting/bread board and place the dough on it. Lightly sprinkle the dough with more flour. Dust your hands with flour as well. Gently knead the dough 10 times by pushing it down and away from you with the heel of your hand, folding it back over itself, turning the dough as you go 1/4 of a turn. Add more flour to the board if the dough starts to stick. Pat the dough into a 9-inch round, flattening the top. Melt butter in a small glass bowl in the microwave. Let cool a few minutes, then brush melted butter on the dough round and sprinkle with the 2 T of sugar. Use a long knife to cut the dough into 12 pie-shaped wedges and transfer to the cookie sheet, leaving 1-inch in between each slice.

Bake 15 - 17 minutes; they will be golden brown.

Note: If you have leftovers scones, freeze them and reheat in a toaster straight from the freezer, they will be delicious!

Fresh Fruit Platter with Oranges, Strawberries, Blueberries and Raspberries.

Fresh Fruit Platter

Number of Servings	16
Serving Dishes	Medium bowl or platter
Preparation Time	15 minutes
Cooking Time	None
Can You Double	Yes
Can You Freeze	No

3 pints strawberries
2 pints raspberries and/or blackberries
2 bunches of red or green grapes w/o seeds
or
3 ripe but firm pears
3 ripe oranges
3 apples
Figs
Lemon juice

This fruit is to accent your guests' plates. In the spring and summer, use seasonal berries. You can choose whatever is ripe and available. In the fall and winter, pears and oranges add nice color and flavor. Slice them thinly, removing the core and stem from the pear. Cut pears and apples at the last minute as they tend to turn brown. Dip in lemon juice to slow down that process.

Lemon Tart with Fresh Fruit

Number of Servings	12
Serving Dishes	Platter or raised cake plate
Preparation Time	20 minutes
Cooking Time	None
Can You Double	No
Can You Freeze	No

1 Frozen Pie Crust
1 c (10 oz) prepared lemon curd
1 1/2 - 2 c mixed berries, citrus segments, kiwis, peaches, nectarines and plums.

Preheat oven according to pie crust package instructions. Bake the pie crust according to the package directions. Transfer to a rack and let cool completely. While pie crust is cooling, slice up selected fresh fruit.

When the crust is cool, evenly spread the lemon curd along the bottom. Arrange fresh fruit in a decorative pattern on top of the lemon curd. Chill. Let guests cut their own pieces to retain the beauty of the tart as long as possible.

Fancy Chocolates and Cookies

Number of Servings	20
Serving Dishes	platter
Preparation Time	10 minutes
Cooking Time	None
Can You Double	Yes
Can You Freeze	No

1 lb assorted fancy chocolates (like truffles from See's Candies)
1 package of fancy cookies (like Pepperidge Farms, Hazelnut Chocolate Spirals)

These small but rich treats round off your tea. Arrange them on a pretty platter with a doily. Use berries to decorate the plate and add contrasting colors. Select fine chocolates and cookies. Go to the candy store for the chocolates, get fancy cookies from the grocery store or local bakery. Make sure you have enough for at least one per guest.

Clotted Cream

Number of Servings	16
Serving Dishes	Small bowl with teaspoon
Preparation Time	10 minutes
Cooking Time	None
Can You Double	Yes
Can You Freeze	No

1 c sour cream
1 c whipping cream, whipped
1/4 c superfine sugar

Before whipping the cream, place beaters in freezer to chill, approximately 30 minutes. This will help the cream whip faster. Whip whipping cream into stiff peaks . Gently stir in the sour cream. Sprinkle superfine sugar into mixture. Gently mix. Spoon into small serving bowl, cover with plastic wrap and refrigerate. Remove from refrigerator and place on table just before guests arrive.

Assorted Seedless Jams and Jellies

Number of Servings	16
Serving Dishes	Small bowls with teaspoons
Preparation Time	5 minutes
Cooking Time	None
Can You Double	Yes
Can You Freeze	No

Offer a selecction of jams and jellies. Favorites include raspberry and blackberry. Use the apricot if you have any leftover from the finger sandwiches. Place in small pretty bowls with small spoons. Cover with plastic wrap and refrigerate. Remove from refrigerator and place on table 1 hour before serving to reduce the chill.

Pesto and Cream Cheese Finger Sandwiches with Cucumber Finger Sandwiches.

Cucumber Finger Sandwiches

Number of Servings	15
Serving Dishes	Platter or raised cake plate
Preparation Time	1 hour 20 minutes
Cooking Time	None
Can You Double	Yes
Can You Freeze	No

1 large cucumber, peeled, sliced paper thin
1/2 tsp salt
2 T white vinegar
1 c unsalted butter, softened (set out on
    counter for about 1 1/2 hours, do not melt)

1/4 c minced fresh tarragon (or 1 T dried)
1/4 c minced fresh chervil (or 1 T dried)
30 thin slices white bread, enough to make 72
    (2x4inch) rectangles
watercress leaves, optional

Put cucumber slices in large bowl. Toss with salt. Sprinkle with vinegar. Toss to mix well. Let stand 1 hour. Drain well in colander. In a small mixing bowl, using a fork, combine butter, tarragon and chervil. To assemble, spread butter over one side of each bread slice. Cover 15 slices with cucumbers, dividing evenly. Close sandwiches. Trim crusts. Cut into 36 rectangles. Arrange on platter, garnished with watercress leaves. If you can't find tarragon and chervil, use minced chives and marjoram or thyme.

Pesto and Cream Cheese Finger Sandwiches

Number of Servings	15
Serving Dishes	Platter or raised cake plate
Preparation Time	1 hour 20 minutes
Cooking Time	None
Can You Double	Yes
Can You Freeze	No

1 (8-oz) package of cream cheese, softened
1/3 c prepared pesto
2 T grated Parmesan Cheese
1 T chopped ripe olives

1 T diced pimentos
1 loaf quality, thinly sliced fresh wheat bread
    (if available at the bakery, have them slice
    an unsliced loaf)

Set cheese out on counter for 1 hour to soften. Blend cream cheese, pesto sauce and parmesan cheese with an electric mixer until smooth. Stir in chopped olive and pimentos. Cover and refrigerate at least one hour. To assemble, spread softened cream cheese filling about an 1/8 of an inch thick. Top with another slice of wheat bread. Trim the crusts off of wheat bread. Cut into four squares.

NOTES

Smoked Salmon and Cream Cheese Finger Sandwiches with
Smoked Ham and Apricot Finger Sandwiches.

Smoked Salmon and Cream Cheese Finger Sandwiches

Number of Servings	16
Serving Dishes	Platter
Preparation Time	45 minutes
Cooking Time	None
Can You Double	Yes
Can You Freeze	No

32 thinly sliced pumpernickel bread
4 oz cream cheese, softened (set out of refrigerator for 30 minutes; room temperature)
1 lb very thinly sliced smoked Salmon
3-4 T dried herbs such as parsley, dill, marjoram

Lay bread slices out on the counter or cutting board. Spread all of the bread slices with a thin layer of cream cheese. Arrange sliced salmon on top of half the slices. Place second slice of bread on top. With a serrated knife, trim the crusts. To serve, cut into squares or triangles and dip one side of the sandwich in herbs then arrange on a platter.

Smoked Ham and Apricot Finger Sandwiches

Number of Servings	16
Serving Dishes	Platter
Preparation Time	15 minutes
Cooking Time	None
Can You Double	Yes
Can You Freeze	No

32 thinly sliced brown or rye bread
8 oz jar apricot jam
1 lbvery thinly sliced smoked ham
4 oz jar Dijon mustard

Lay bread slices out on the counter or cutting board. Spread half the bread slices with a thin layer of apricot jam. Arrange sliced ham on top. Spread the remaining bread slices with a thin layer of Dijon mustard and cover the ham. With a serrated knife, trim the crusts. To serve, cut into squares or triangles and arrange on a platter with the Smoked Salmon sandwiches.

The Tea Beverages

The stores have a large assortment of teas. It can almost be overwhelming. We would recommend staying clear of all the strange or exotic varieties and stick with simple tried and true classics, unless of course you are a tea connoisseur and have a favorite flavor. Classic teas include: Earl Grey, English Breakfast, Darjeeling and Orange Pekoe; make sure one of the varieties is decaffeinated for guests that don't need the caffeine rush!

How to Brew a Great Cup of Tea For making tea, don't use tea bags in a mug with hot water. Make tea properly by:

1. Using loose tea 1 tsp or a quality bag tea for every cup (use one less tea bag)
2. Boiling fresh cold water (bottled if tap water is odd tasting)
3. Use a teapot, preheating it by running it under and filling it with hot tap water; remove water when tea water boils
4. Place bags, loose tea, or tea ball filled with loose tea in the pot and pour in boiling water
5. Steep the tea for 3 to 5 minutes
6. Gently stir tea before pouring it through a tea strainer; if you used tea bags, remove them

Iced Tea with a Splash This is a punch-like iced tea recipe. This beverage goes quickly, so make a few batches ahead of time and store in pitchers in your refrigerator. You can make it with or without alcohol. If you do add alcohol, you will need to reduce the sugar by 1/2 cup.

Note: *Make a sugar syrup for easy mixing into cold drinks. Just mix equal parts sugar and water, simmer until sugar is dissolved, about 5 minutes. Store in a covered jar until ready to use. It will keep indefinitely in the refrigerator.*

Put 6 Constant Comment or other orange spice tea bags in a nonmetal heatproof container. If you don't have one, you can two-cup glass measuring cup with a spoon sticking out of it. Add 2 cups of boiling water. Let tea steep until it is cool. Wring out the tea bags and discard. Pour tea into a large pitcher. Add the following:

1 6 ou can frozen lemonade concentrate (use 1/2 can of a 12 oz can)
1 6 ou can frozen orange juice concentrate
1 1/2 c superfine sugar (remember to reduce by 1/2 cup if adding Grand Marnier)
7 c cold water
1 c orange liqueur (Grand Marnier, optional)
1/2 c vodka (optional)

Stir well. Add sliced oranges and lemons for garnish. Chill until very cold, pour over ice in glasses and garnish with orange slices.

The Grocery List - Tea Buffet

Two weeks before the party

- ❑ 1 frozen pie crust
- ❑ 1 6 oz frozen lemonade
- ❑ 1 6 oz frozen orange juice
- ❑ 1 box superfine sugar
- ❑ 1 box of brown sugar
- ❑ 1 bag sugar
- ❑ 1 sm box sugar cubes
- ❑ 2 c flour
- ❑ Baking powder
- ❑ Salt
- ❑ White wine vinegar
- ❑ 1 1/2 c unsalted butter
- ❑ Small chunk of parmesan cheese
- ❑ 1 4 oz jar of Dijon mustard
- ❑ 1 sm can chopped black olives
- ❑ 1 sm jar of diced pimentos
- ❑ 3/4 c dried cranberries
- ❑ Honey, small jar (8 oz)
- ❑ 2 sm jars of assorted jams and jellies (raspberry, boysenberry etc., 8 oz)
- ❑ 1 8 oz jar apricot jam
- ❑ 1 jar (10 oz) prepared Lemon Curd
- ❑ Loose tea (Earl Grey, Darjeeling, Orange Pekoe)
- ❑ 1 box Constant Comment tea
- ❑ Fancy cookies (Pepperidge farm or bakery)
- ❑ Orange liquor (Grand Marnier or Curacao) optional
- ❑ Vodka - optional
- ❑ Candles
- ❑ Matches

Day before the party

- ❑ 16 oz half & half
- ❑ 1% milk
- ❑ 2 c heavy cream (whipping)
- ❑ 1 c sour cream
- ❑ 1 8 oz cream cheese
- ❑ 1/3 c prepared pesto
- ❑ 1 lb thinly sliced smoked ham (ask butcher to slice it "paper thin" or select the most thinly sliced packaged ham).
- ❑ 1 cucumber
- ❑ 1/4 c fresh tarragon or 1 sm dried tarragon
- ❑ 1/4 c fresh Chervil or 1 sm dried chervil
- ❑ Fresh watercress leaves
- ❑ 4 oranges
- ❑ 3 lemons
- ❑ 2 c of fruit: berries, citrus, kiwi, peaches (for tart topping
- ❑ Fresh fruit (3 pints strawberries, 1 pint raspberries, or 3 ripe pears and 3 oranges)
- ❑ 1 loaf of thinly sliced white bread
- ❑ 1 loaf of thinly sliced pumpernickel or a second loaf of whole wheat
- ❑ 1 loaf whole wheat bread, thinly sliced (30 pieces)
- ❑ 1 loaf brown or rye bread, thinly sliced (30 pieces)

The Time Line ~ Tea Buffet

Four weeks before the party
- ❑ Determine budget
- ❑ Identify location, determine date/time/ambiance
- ❑ Compile guest list
- ❑ Purchase invitations
- ❑ Address and mail invitations (especially at holiday time, it is important to mail your invitations early because friends get booked)

Select what your are going to wear, take any items to the dry cleaners for cleaning and/or pressing.

Two weeks before party
- ❑ Make cranberry orange scones (wrap tight and freeze) or order from bakery or tea house
- ❑ Assess party set-up needs: linens/serving pieces/dinnerware etc. (get everything out, wash what needs to be cleaned, polish silver if necessary etc. This can be very time consuming so don't delay. You will also find that if you need to rent or borrow something, you will have adequate time to do so.
- ❑ Place rental order if needed (chairs/dinnerware) or call family to borrow pieces
- ❑ Main grocery shopping (see shopping list)

One week before party
- ❑ Pick up serving pieces (plastic/borrowed)
- ❑ If hosting the party outside: Mow the lawns, weed, spruce up potted plants by removing struggling plants and adding fresh, vibrant plants. Plant brightly colored plants in pots for the centerpieces of your dining tables and the serving table (baby roses or gerber daisies are nice), wash down the patio area.
- ❑ Thoroughly clean the house (see home preparation section)
- ❑ Pick up 1 lb of fancy chocolates

One day before party
- ❑ Defrost scones or pick up scones from bakery/tea house
- ❑ Purchase perishables (see "last minute" grocery list)
- ❑ Make fruit tart, cover and refrigerate
- ❑ Brew tea for spiked orange iced tea, store in a nonmetallic container, covered in the refrigerator
- ❑ Prepare cream cheese pesto filling. Store in sealed plastic container.
- ❑ Set table with linens and decor (not perishables), set out serving pieces and utensils (if an indoor party)
- ❑ Refrigerate Champagne
- ❑ Put assorted jams and jellies in serving bowls. Cover with plastic wrap and refrigerate.
- ❑ Make clotted cream, place in serving bowl, cover with plastic wrap and refrigerate.

The Time Line - Tea Buffet Continued

Day of party (3 hours before guests arrive)
- ☐ Remove cream cheese and pesto filling from refrigerator to soften
- ☐ Make tea sandwiches, platter, cover with a damp (not wet!) cloth and refrigerate
- ☐ Pick up/have delivered rentals if required
- ☐ Slice lemons, arrange on small plate, cover with plastic and refrigerate
- ☐ Rinse fresh fruit, let drain, arrange in bowl
- ☐ Platter cookies and wrap in plastic, set on table
- ☐ Arrange fancy chocolates on a pretty platter, cover and keep in a cool place until ready to serve
- ☐ Make spiked orange iced tea
- ☐ If hosting party outside, hose off patio, sweep off extra water and set tables. Cover tables with sheets to keep off dust and debris.

Day of party (1 hour before guests arrive)
- ☐ Get yourself ready for the arrival of your guests

Day of party (30 Minutes before guests arrive)
- ☐ Preheat oven to bake scones
- ☐ Place jams and jellies, honey and sugar on the serving table or tables where guests are sitting
- ☐ Boil water and fill tea pots with water to warm
- ☐ Put on selected music, (tapes and CD's work best for continuous play)
- ☐ Make one last review of the table, check for serving utensils etc.

Day of party (10 minutes before guests arrive)
- ☐ Place fruit, tart, sandwiches, clotted cream, cream and/or milk, sliced lemons, and fancy chocolates on the serving table
- ☐ Boil water for tea
- ☐ Light candles

Make appointment to get your nails done the day prior to your tea party.

From top center, Tomato Salad, Tortilla Chips & Guacamole, Black Beans, Rice, Coconut Cornbread, Queijandinhas, Flan, Rice and Marinated Shrimp, Chicken and Beef Kabobs.

The Brazilian Bar-B-Que Buffet

It's Sunday and you've invited a gang of people over to watch the "big game" on TV. Bar-B-Que's are pretty typical for this type of gathering, but we dare you to add a little ethnic splash with this buffet. Brazil is the world's largest grower and the biggest consumer of beans and the national dish is feijoada; a rich, liquid stew of black beans in which several kinds of meat are submerged. We've included this authentic dish as well as a modified version of churrascaria - meat roasted on a spit over a fire. In our menu, we offer grilled marinated meats & shrimp cooked on your Bar-B-Que or broiled in your oven. This menu consists of mostly authentic recipes, but go ahead and add some tortilla chips, guacamole & salsa. Brazilian food is healthy, flavorful and simple to prepare. Cold beers and margaritas go well with this menu. Blend up some lime and strawberry margaritas for your guests. Then sit back and enjoy the game!

What You Need For This Party:

Serving Pieces:
3 small glass or crystal bowls
1 glass pedestal or standard bowl
2 oval or round platters
1 large basket w/ a pretty napkin to line
1 wide shallow bowl/casserole
3 large pitchers
20 dinner-size plates
20 forks
20 tall glasses
40 napkins
large tub or ice chest for beer
15 margarita glasses

Cooking Utensils:
large mixing bowl
medium mixing bowl
small mixing bowl
1 loaf pan
cutting board
knives (serrated, chef and paring)
fork, rubber spatula, wooden spoon
measuring spoons, cups and glass measurer
wooden or metal skewers
6-8 qt stock pot
1 1/2 qt sauce pan
wire rack
2-quart Jello or bundt cake mold
blender
large oven proof pan, e.g. turkey roaster

Marinated Chicken, Shrimp and Beef Kabobs.

Marinated Chicken and Beef Kabobs

Number of Servings	12
Serving Dishes	Platter
Preparation Time	1 hour
Cooking Time	About 10 minutes
Can You Double	Yes
Can You Freeze	No

3-4 lbs beef (filet mignon or similar quality beef)
3-4 lbs chicken breasts, skinless & boneless

Brazilian Garlic-Lime Marinade
18-20 cloves garlic, minced (you can also use minced garlic from a jar from your grocery store)
3 c fresh lime and/or lemon juice
1 c dry white wine
6 T red wine vinegar
2 bunch basil, cilantro, dill, parsley, oregano, or a mix of all, finely chopped to yield 1 cup
1 bunch green onions, (white & green parts), trimmed and finely chopped to yield 1/2 cup
2-4 tsp hot sauce or Tabasco sauce (optional)
salt (coarse) & pepper to taste
24 wooden skewers

Cut the beef & chicken into large bite size chunks. Mix all ingredients in a bowl and whisk until blended. In separate bags, put chunks of cubed beef into a large plastic storage Ziploc bag and pour marinade into same bag. While sealing bag, try to press out as much air as possible. When sealed, put into refrigerator for 1 – 2 hours to marinate. Do the same with the cubed chicken. Meanwhile, soak the wooden skewers in water for 15 minutes. When ready, skewer several pieces of meat onto the wooden skewers and cook several minutes on each side.

Special Note: The churrascaria is a grill and has become a popular type of restaurant especially in California. At a churrascaria, large cuts of meat are roasted on a spit over the fire and then divided after cooking. Brazilians do not cut off fat from meat before grilling, for this both aids the cooking and adds flavor. Cut away surplus fat after cooking. For a party, the host will cook many cuts and types of meat, including chicken, pork, and sausages. White meats, chicken and pork, are always marinated first in a mixture of lime juice, minced onion and garlic, chopped parsley or cilantro, and seasoning to taste.   Generally, beef is just salted (brined) and peppered. Here, we marinated beef, chicken & shrimp for this party.

Marinated Shrimp Kabobs

Number of Servings	12
Serving Dishes	Large platter
Preparation Time	1 hour
Cooking Time	About 5 minutes
Can You Double	Yes
Can You Freeze	No

3-4 lbs of jumbo shrimp (minimum of 36 pieces)
8-10 cloves garlic, minced (you can also use minced garlic from a jar from your grocery store)
1 ½ c fresh lime and/or lemon juice
1 bunch cilantro, finely chopped to yield ½ cup
1 bunch green onions, (white & green parts), trimmed and finely chopped to yield ¼ cup
salt (coarse) & pepper to taste
20 wooden skewers

Clean shrimp. Mix all ingredients, except shrimp, in a bowl and whisk until blended. Put shrimp into a large plastic storage zip lock bag and add marinade. While sealing bag, press out as much air as possible. Refrigerate 1 – 2 hours. When ready, skewer several pieces of shrimp onto wooden skewers and cook a few minutes on each side. Shrimp will cook quickly, watch carefully. Cook the shrimp last to avoid over cooking.

Queijadinhas (Little Cheese Custards)

Number of Servings	24
Serving Dishes	Cupcake mold to bake; platter to serve
Preparation Time	10 minutes
Cooking Time	30 minutes
Can You Double	Yes
Can You Freeze	No

1 15 oz can condensed milk   1 c grated coconut
2 large egg yolks   2 tsp freshly grated Parmesan cheese

Preheat oven to 400 degrees. Mix all ingredients in a large bowl. Spray the cupcake molds with non-stick spray. Fill the molds with the mixture. Place the cupcake molds into a roasting pan. Place the roasting pan with the cupcake molds in the oven on the first rack, then pour in the boiling water to the halfway point of the cupcake pan. Bake for 30 minutes. Cool in pan for 10 minutes, remove from cupcake pan (this can be a little tricky, so be patient) and place on a wire rack to cool completely. Store in an airtight container in the refrigerator.

Tortilla Chips and Guacamole

Number of Servings	20
Serving Dishes	Baskets and small bowls
Preparation Time	5 minutes
Cooking Time	None
Can You Double	No
Can You Freeze	No

1 2 lb bag of tortilla chips
2 c (16 oz) prepared guacamole (look for guacamole made with real avocados - check the freezer section)
2-3 assorted salsas, varying both spiciness and temperature as well as texture; can be jars or fresh from the deli section

This is a quick appetizer that will go well with the margaritas. You can place this on the buffet table if you are ready to serve immediately when your guests arrive, or place on coffee tables with small plates and napkins so guests can enjoy with their pre-dinner drink. If the guacamole is frozen, remove from the freezer and place in the refrigerator the night before the party so it can defrost. Check it a few hours before the party. If it is still frozen, take out of the refrigerator to thaw.

Coconut Cornbread

Number of Servings	12
Serving Dishes	Platter
Preparation Time	20 minutes
Cooking Time	30-35 minutes
Can You Double	No
Can You Freeze	No

1 Marie Calendars Cornbread
3/4 c coconut milk
3/4 c water
1/2 tsp cinnamon

Mix 1/2 tsp cloves
1/2 tsp nutmeg
1 bag shredded coconut (optional)

Preheat oven to 400 degrees. Mix all ingredients in a large bowl. Spray a loaf pan with vegetable spray. Pour batter into loaf pan. Bake for 30 to 35 minutes. Do not overbake or the bread will be dry. Cool in pan for 10 minutes. Remove from loaf pan and place on a wire rack right side up to cool.

Fresh Tomato Salad with Red Wine Vinaigrette

Fresh Tomato Salad with Red Wine Viniagrette

Number of Servings	12-15
Serving Dishes	Clear glass bowl or pedestal bowl
Preparation Time	15 minutes
Cooking Time	None
Can You Double	Yes
Can You Freeze	No

24 roma tomatoes or 12 large vine ripe tomatoes
1 bottle (24 oz) red wine vinaigrette dressing
1 bunch green onions, sliced into thin slivers

1 T sugar
Salt & black pepper to taste

Rinse tomatoes. Slice into bite size chunks (about 1 inch pieces) and place into mixing bowl. Add sliced green onions (white & some green parts), reserve some for garnish, and half the bottle of vinaigrette to tomatoes in the bowl. Toss together until well blended. Add a little sugar, which helps to cut the acidity. Add salt and pepper. Toss again and taste. Keep in refrigerator until ready to serve. Transfer to pretty glass serving bowl and garnish with remaining green onions.

Fiesta Rice

Number of Servings	12-15
Serving Dishes	Casserole dish
Preparation Time	10 minutes
Cooking Time	20-25 minutes
Can You Double	Yes, this recipe is already doubled
Can You Freeze	No

2 T sunflower or olive oil
1 medium onion, chopped
2 c long grain rice
1 c green, red, yellow and/
  or orange bell peppers, cut into 1/2 inch pieces

1 clove garlic, minced
4 c boiling water
1 tsp salt
1 tsp white pepper

In a frying pan, saute onions in oil until onions are translucent. Add the garlic and cook for one more minute. Add rice and bell peppers to onion mixture in pot. Stir rice for a minute over medium heat until the rice has a white coating. Add 4 cups of boiling water to pan and bring water back to boil. Lower heat to simmer; cover pan and cook for approximately 20-25 minutes. At that time, take a fork and poke through rice to the bottom of the pan and make sure that all water has been absorbed. Keep covered and remove from heat for a five minutes. Remove the lid and let stand 5 more minutes. Transfer to serving dish. Sprinkle additional pieces of bell pepper on top for garnish.

Black Bean Stew

Black Bean Stew

Number of Servings	12-15
Serving Dishes	Tureen or other large bowl-platter
Preparation Time	15 minutes
Cooking Time	3 hours
Can You Double	Yes, this recipe is a double batch
Can You Freeze	Yes

2 lb (5 cups) dried black beans
1 ham bone or package of ham hocks (You can ask the butcher at your market or the deli counter if they have a ham bone that you can purchase or if your neighborhood has a honey baked ham store, then you can purchase a ham bone from them.)
1-2 lbs Italian sausage or Linguica sausage
1 large onion, minced
4 garlic cloves, crushed, then chopped (you can also use minced garlic from a jar)
1 bunch of scallions, white & green parts, chopped
2 bay leaves
salt & black pepper to taste
hot sauce (optional)

Rinse the beans and discard any discolored ones or any small rocks. Soak in water overnight in a bowl. Transfer the beans and their water into a large stewing pot, adding more water to bring the level to 3" above the beans. Do not add salt at this stage, as it will harden the beans. Bring to a boil and boil rapidly for 10 minutes, then lower the heat. Beans will need to simmer for 2-3 hours, stirring occasionally. Once you have begun the simmering, then add the ham bone/hocks and bay leaves into pot. Cook for an hour.

Add sauteed onions & scallions, garlic and sausage. Sausage can be cooked separately or added to the beans while simmering. Simmer for another hour.

After a couple of hours of simmering, test beans for doneness (mushy). At this point, you can season with salt & pepper to taste. The beans can be soupy or if you want a thicker consistency, then take out a few ladles of beans and crush them with the back of a wooden spoon, return them to the pot. This will thicken the sauce.

Transfer to a tureen or other serving dish. A ladle is the best utensil to spoon out the beans.

Flan

Flan

Number of Servings	8-10
Serving Dishes	2 qt. jello or bundt cake mold and a large platter
Preparation Time	15 minutes
Cooking Time	90 minutes
Can You Double	Yes
Can You Freeze	No

14 oz can sweetened condensed milk
28 oz whole milk (use the empty can of condensed milk as a measuring cup, just fill it twice!)
3 eggs
1 tsp vanilla extract
1-1/2 c of sugar

Preheat oven to 325 degrees. In a blender, blend condensed milk through the vanilla. Make sure all ingredients are incorporated, scrape down the sides of the blender with a rubber spatula.

For the caramel sauce, measure sugar into a small, heavy saucepan. Set the sugar over medium heat. Wait for about a minute before stirring the sugar. Using a wooden spoon, stir sugar constantly. The sugar will gradually melt into a clear syrup. Be mindful to scrap the sides of the pan if the sugar crystallizes. Eventually, the heat will melt it all. When the sugar has melted, cook a little bit longer until it gets to a nice caramel brown color. When done, pour your caramel syrup in the bottom of your mold. Pick up the mold and gently swirl the caramel syrup around the bottom and sides of the mold.

Pour your milk/egg mixture from your blender into the caramel-lined mold. When you pour your mixture over the hardened caramel syrup, you will hear the caramel crackle a little. Find a larger pan (perhaps a turkey roaster) and fill it with water about 1/3 way. Place your mold in the water bath, the water should be halfway up the sides of the mold. Bake for 90 minutes. Check on your flan for doneness by giving the mold a slight jiggle. If it jiggles too much, then bake it for another 5-10 minutes. If it just gives slightly then insert a clean, smooth knife it in the middle and if it comes out clean, then it is ready.

Take the flan out of the oven and let cool for a few minutes. Cover the mold with plastic wrap and place in the refrigerator for at least 4 hours. It can be kept in the refrigerator, in the mold, for up to 2 days. When you are ready to un-mold, take a smooth slender knife and go around the edges of the mold. You can also dip your mold briefly in hot water. Place your platter over the top of the mold and invert your mold onto the platter. Make sure that your serving platter is large enough to catch all the caramel that will cascade over the sides of your flan when it comes out of your mold. You can garnish with shredded coconut, slivered almonds, mint leaves, or even fruit.

Assorted Mexican Beers with Lime, Mango and Strawberry Margaritas.

The Bar-B-Que Beverages

Fruit Margaritas:
8 oz bag of frozen mango, papaya or strawberries
3 oz Tequila
1 oz Triple Sec
7 oz margarita mix
Crushed ice

To make a pitcher of fruit margaritas, fill 1/2 the blender with frozen fruit. Add the tequila, triple sec and margarita mix. Add enough crushed ice to fill the blender 3/4 full. Place lid on blender and begin blending in small bursts until mixture is smooth. Add additional ice if needed. This will make approximately 6 single sized servings.

Lime Margaritas
1/2 can limeade
8 ou Tequila
4 ou Triple Sec
Crushed ice

To make a pitcher of lime margaritas, place 1/2 can of limeade in a blender, then fill the blender with ice. Pour tequila and triple sec over the ice. (You may add 4-8 oz of water to reduce the tartness of the margarita). Place lid on the blender and start blending using small bursts to begin mixing and then continue until smooth. This will make approximately 6 single sized servings.

Assorted Mexican Beers Corona, Dos Equis, Pacifico, Tecate, Carte Blanca.

Passion Fruit Iced Tea Paradise brand iced tea makes a passion fruit iced tea. The box recipe calls for 4 cups of water per tea bag. Make according to box directions and once cooled, place in refrigerator at least two hours. Add sliced oranges, lemons and limes for color with ice to the pitcher when ready to serve.

Lemonade Homemade is the best, but frozen will do! Make according to directions on can. Add sliced lemons and ice to the pitcher before serving.

The Grocery List - Brazilian Bar-B-Que

Two weeks before the party
- ❒ 1 16 oz bag black beans
- ❒ 2 c long grain rice (uncooked)
- ❒ 1 (12 oz) bottle red wine vinegar
- ❒ 2 cans sweetened condensed milk
- ❒ vanilla and/or almond extract
- ❒ salt
- ❒ fresh ground pepper
- ❒ sugar
- ❒ 2 cans Limeade
- ❒ 2 cans Lemonade
- ❒ 20 oz bottle tequila (select a premium brand)
- ❒ 1 bottle Triple Sec
- ❒ 1 large bottle Sweet & Sour Mix (Margarita Mix)
- ❒ assorted Mexican beer
- ❒ 1 box Paradise Passion Fruit tea
- ❒ frozen strawberries
- ❒ frozen mangos
- ❒ frozen papayas

Day before the party
- ❒ 2-3 onions, chopped (equivalent to 2 cups)
- ❒ 1 bunch green onions, chopped
- ❒ 3 bell peppers (green, red & yellow or orange)
- ❒ 8-10 roma tomatoes
- ❒ 2 lbs beef (filet mignon or new york steak)
- ❒ 2 lbs boneless, skinless chicken
- ❒ 2 lbs shrimp (uncooked; deveined if you can find)
- ❒ 1/2 gallon whole milk or heavy cream
- ❒ 6 large or extra large eggs
- ❒ 6 limes
- ❒ 6 lemons
- ❒ 2 oranges
- ❒ 3 garlic cloves

The Time Line - Brazilian Bar-B-Que

Four weeks before the party
- ❏ Determine budget
- ❏ Identify location, determine date, time and ambiance
- ❏ Compile guest list
- ❏ Purchase invitations
- ❏ Address and mail invitations

Two weeks before party
- ❏ Assess party set up needs: linens, serving pieces, dinnerware
- ❏ Place rental order if needed (chairs/dinnerware) or call family to borrow pieces
- ❏ Main grocery shopping (see shopping list)

One week before party
- ❏ Pick up serving pieces (plastic/borrowed)
- ❏ If hosting the party outside: Mow the lawns, weed, spruce up potted plants by removing struggling plants and adding fresh, vibrant plants. Plant brightly colored plants in pots for the centerpieces of your tables (baby roses or gerber daisies are nice) and the serving table, wash down the patio area.
- ❏ Thoroughly clean the house (see home preparation section)
- ❏ Shop for dry/canned goods

One day before party
- ❏ Purchase perishables (see "last minute" grocery list)
- ❏ Cut up meats (beef and chicken). Devein shrimp if necessary. Make beef marinade and marinate beef.
- ❏ Chop onions and bell peppers coarsely, seal in plastic baggies and store in refrigerator.
- ❏ Make flan. When cooled after baking, cover mold and store in refrigerator overnight. (Do not freeze!)
- ❏ Sort through bad of beans for bad beans or small pebbles; Place beans in a large stock pot and cover with water; soak overnight.
- ❏ Set table with linens, serving pieces, utensils and decor (not perishables),

Day of party 4 hours before guests arrive
- ❏ Make tomato salad; refrigerate.
- ❏ Make marinade for chicken; marinate chicken.
- ❏ Start cooking the beans.
- ❏ Rinse the rice in a colander and let dry.

Day of party 4 hours before
- ❏ Make tomato salad; refrigerate.
- ❏ Make marinade for chicken; marinate chicken.
- ❏ Start cooking the beans.
- ❏ Rinse the rice in a colander and let dry.

Day of party 1 1/2 hours before guests arrive
- ❏ Marinate shrimp.
- ❏ Prepare the rice.
- ❏ Soak skewers; skewer meats and shrimp
- ❏ Grill meats; grill shrimp last!

From top center: "Grilled" Artichokes with Aioli Sauce, Peach Bread Pudding, Dirty Rice with Chicken, Cheese Stuffed Jalapenos, Olive Tepenade on Fresh French Bread, Assorted Grilled Sausages and Shrimp, Mango Salsa and assorted Sweet Potato Chips.

The Casual Cajun Buffet

This party was inspired by a trip we took to New Orleans. One of our friends took us to the great old establishment, and we mean old - building circa 1700's and although we didn't eat there, we enjoyed the ambiance and the Hurricanes. This party is best at night and best suited for adults. We set the tables in black and used accents of purple, gold, green and magenta - like the mardi gras beads New Orleans is famous for. We turned the lights down real low, lit a bunch of candles and offered our friends and family southern cooking and beverages. So put on the jazz and blues music, light the candles, don a mask if you dare and don't forget to leave room for dessert; the Peach Bread Pudding with Southern Comfort Cream and Caramel Whisky Sauce is worth the indulgence!

What You Need For This Party:

Serving Pieces:
3 small glass or crystal bowls
1 glass pedestal or standard bowl
1 glass or crystal bowl
3 oval or round platters
2 rectangular platters
1 wide shallow bowl/casserole
9 x 13 inch casserole
1 punch bowl with ladle
20 dinner-size plates
20 forks
20 tall glasses
40 napkins
large tub or ice chest
15 margarita glasses
1 small serving spoon
1 large serving spoon
1 gravy boat or small pitcher

Cooking Utensils:
large mixing bowl
medium mixing bowl
small mixing bowl
cutting board
knives (serrated, chef and paring)
rubber spatula, wooden spoon
measuring spoons, cups and glass measurer
6-8 quart stock pot
1 1/2 quart sauce pan
blender
broil pan
baking sheet
colander
large zip lock baggies

Assorted Grilled Sausages and Shrimp with Mango Salsa.

Boiled Shrimp

Number of Servings	12
Serving Dishes	Platter
Preparation Time	20 minutes
Cooking Time	None
Can You Double	No
Can You Freeze	No

2 lbs of Shrimp
1 box Zataran's Crab Boil in a Bag
2 large lemons, sliced
1 tsp cayenne pepper

You can purchase raw shrimp either peeled or unpeeled. Feel free to purchase unpeeled, just cut the back of the shrimp shell so that your guests can more easily peel off the shell. If you purchased peeled shrimp, make sure it comes with the tail on, for handling. Either type of shrimp will need to be deviened if not done so already. Follow the directions on the crab boil box. Be very careful not to overcook the shrimp. They cook very quickly and are hard and tough if overdone.

Assorted Sausages

Number of Servings	12
Serving Dishes	Platter
Preparation Time	20 minutes
Cooking Time	None
Can You Double	No
Can You Freeze	No

2 lbs of assorted sausages - hot links

Cajun means spicy, not Italian, so purchase a variety of Louisiana hot links. Farmer John and Aidells are brands you can find at your local market. We recommend grilling or broiling the sausage. If you would like, you can cook the sausage ahead of time and warm them up in a microwave before you are ready to serve. Platter sausage in an oven safe dish and cover with foil to keep warm until ready to eat.

"Grilled" Artichokes with Aioli Sauce.

"Grilled" Artichokes with Aioli Sauce

Number of Servings	12
Serving Dishes	Large, wide low casserole dish and small glass bowl
Preparation Time	20 minutes
Cooking Time	None
Can You Double	No
Can You Freeze	No

12 artichokes	2-3 oz Worcestershire sauce
1/4 c sesame oil	1 c mayonnaise
1/4 c olive oil	1 stick (1/2 c) butter, melted
3 T honey	1 T crushed garlic
2 T lemon juice	
2 tsp season salt	

To make sauce, mix oils, honey, lemon juice, salt, worcestershire sauce, and mayonnaise. Cover and refrigerate. To prepare artichokes, cut artichokes into quarters and steam, boil or microwave until they are tender and the leaves are easy to pull off; approximately 45 minutes. Turn on oven broiler. Place artichokes in a large casserole dish. Mix butter and chopped garlic. Brush over artichokes. Place artichokes in broiler. Baste artichokes with garlic butter until artichokes are crispy. Serve artichokes with aioli sauce on the side.

Appetizers: Jalepeno Poppers, Olive Tepenade, Assorted Breads

Number of Servings	12
Serving Dishes	2 Platters
Preparation Time	20 minutes
Cooking Time	10 minutes (according to package instructions)
Can You Double	Yes
Can You Freeze	Poppers and bread yes, Tepenade, no

These items are pre made and purchased. The poppers need to be cooked. Follow the instructions on the package. Platter and serve immediately.

Olive tepenade can be purchased in the deli section. Un-mold from container onto a small pretty plate or bowl. Arrange small slices of bread on a plate or in a basket.

Dirty Rice with Chicken.

Dirty Rice with Chicken

Number of Servings	12
Serving Dishes	Casserole
Preparation Time	15 minutes
Cooking Time	25 minutes
Can You Double	Already doubled
Can You Freeze	No

2 boxes of Zatarain's Dirty Rice
2 lbs ground chicken
5 c water

4 Tbl vegetable oil
1/2 c finely diced red and or green bell peppers

We adapted a box recipe for this dish. If you cannot find the Zatarain brand, look for other packaged rice kits from another maker. Be aware that packaged foods can be salty; adjust seasoning as needed. Lightly brown the ground chicken. In a large (5 qt) sauce pan or stock pot, combine water and oil; bring to a boil. Add Zatarain's rice mix and chicken, return to a boil. Reduce heat, stir, cover and simmer over low heat for 20 minutes. Add diced bell peppers and continue cooking for another 5 - 10 minutes. Remove from heat. Let stand 5 minutes and fluff with a fork.

Mango Relish

Number of Servings	12
Serving Dishes	Pedestal bowl or glass/crystal bowl
Preparation Time	20 minutes
Cooking Time	None
Can You Double	No
Can You Freeze	No

2 medium-size ripe mangos (about 1 lb), peeled, seeded, and chopped (about 1 1/2 cups)
1/2 c shallots finely chopped
1/4 c seeded fresh Anaheim peppers cut into 1/4 inch pieces
1/4 c seeded fresh jalapeno chile peppers (red preferably, or green) cut into 1/4 inch pieces
2 T medium-hot pepper sauce
3 T rice vinegar
1/4 c vinegar
1/2 c loosely packed finely chopped fresh cilantro leaves
1/2 c seeded green bell peppers cut into 1/4 inch pieces
1/2 tsp salt
3 T white balsamic vinegar
1/4 c syrup (cane, fruit or maple, but not pancake)

Combine all ingredients in a medium bowl and stir until well blended. Cover and refrigerate at least 4 hours, preferably overnight. Refrigerate any leftovers. Relish will last one week in the refrigerator.

NOTES

Pound Cake with Fresh Raspberries, Blueberries and Strawberries

Pound Cake with Fresh Berries

Number of Servings	16
Serving Dishes	Platter or raised cake plate, small bowl for cream with spoon; medium crystal bowl for berries
Preparation Time	20 minutes
Cooking Time	0
Can You Double	Yes
Can You Freeze	No

2 store bought pound cakes
2 baskets of strawberries
2 baskets of raspberries
2 baskets of blackberries
1 basket of blueberries
1/4 c sugar
1 carton of Cool Whip topping or 1 can of whipped cream

Wash berries and place on paper towels to dry. Hull strawberries (remove stem) and slice. Combine all the berries in a bowl, add the sugar, stirring gently (you don't want to squish the berries) and refrigerate until ready to serve. Slice the pound cake in 1/2 inch thickness; platter, cover with plastic wrap to keep cake from drying out; set aside. When ready to serve, remove berries from mixing bowl and carefully spoon into a serving bowl. If using Cool Whip, transfer the Cool Whip to a serving bowl. Don't forget serving spoons for the berries and whip cream.

Peach Bread Pudding

Peach Bread Pudding with Southern Comfort Cream and Whisky Caramel Sauces

Number of Servings	12
Serving Dishes	9 x 13 inch casserole, small bowl for cream with spoon; gravy boat w/spoon for sauce
Preparation Time	20 minutes
Cooking Time	50-60 minutes
Can You Double	No
Can You Freeze	No

Bread Pudding

1/2 loaf of brioche, (or day old thick cut french bread) cut into 1-inch cubes w/ crusts removed
   (8 cups)
1/2 c butter, melted
6 T sugar
2 T cinnamon
8 medium peaches (or 3 cans of peaches) peeled, pitted
2 T Peach Schnapps
2/3 c whipping cream
2/3 c milk (don't use nonfat)
1/4 c sugar
1 tsp cinnamon
3 eggs, beaten

Preheat oven to 350 degrees. Mix sugar and two T cinnamon. Toss cubed bread with melted butter and cinnamon sugar mix. Place on a baking sheet and toast until light brown, approximately 10 minutes. Remove from oven and reduce temperature to 325 degrees. Peel, pit and chop 2 peaches and combine with Schnapps in a bowl. Add cream. Cover and refrigerate. In a small saucepan, bring milk, sugar and cinnamon to a boil. Place eggs in a stainless steel bowl and slowly drizzle milk mixture over eggs while whisking rapidly. Stir into cream mixture. Peel, pit and chop remaining 6 peaches and add to peach and cream mixture. Stir together bread cubes and peach mixture until liquid is absorbed.

Butter a 9 x 13 inch casserole dish. Coat with remaining cinnamon-sugar mixture. Pour in bread pudding mixture. Bake for 50 to 60 minutes.

Southern Comfort Cream and Caramel-Whisky Sauces

Southern Comfort Cream
1 c whipping cream
1 c half and half
1/2 vanilla bean
5 egg yolks
1/2 c sugar
2 T Southern Comfort

Place cream and half and half in a stainless steel saucepan. Split vanilla bean and scrape seeds into cream mixture. Add vanilla pod. Bring to a boil. Whisk egg yolks and sugar in a stainless steel bowl 2 minutes. Slowly add hot cream mixture, whisking, 1 minute. Return mixture to saucepan. Cook over low heat, stirring constantly, until cream coats the back of a spoon, about 5 minutes. Do not allow to boil or it will curdle. Strain mixture through a sieve and cool completely. Add Southern Comfort. Pour into an airtight container and store in refrigerator until day of party. To serve, pour cream into a gravy boat for guest to add to bread pudding.

Caramel-Whisky Sauce
1 1/2 c sugar
2/3 c water
1/4 c butter
1/4 c (2 ounces) cream cheese
1/4 c Irish whisky
1/4 c milk

Combine the sugar and water in a saucepan over medium heat, cook and stir until sugar dissolves (watch so the sugar does not burn). Cook for an additional 15 minutes or until golden brown (do not stir). Remove from heat. Stirring with a whisk, add the butter and cream cheese (the mixture will be hot and bubble vigorously). Cool slightly, then stir in whisky and milk. Serve warm from a gravy boat with a spoon.

The Beverages

We are giving you a selection of drinks to make. Don't feel you need to make all of them for one party. Remember to keep things simple for yourself and your guests!

Southern Hurricane
1 1/2 oz Southern Comfort (or your favorite bourbon)
1/2 oz grenadine
lemon-lime soda
sliced oranges
Maraschino cherries

Fill a tall glass with ice. Add bourbon and grenadine. Fill glass with lemon-lime soda. Garnish with an orange slice and cherry.

Southern Frost
1 1/2 oz Southern Comfort (or your favorite bourbon)
2 oz cranberry juice
2 oz of gingerale
fresh/frozen cranberries if available

Fill a tall glass with ice. Add bourbon and cranberry juice. Fill glass with gingerale. Garnish with a few cranberries.

Open House Punch
1 (750 ml) bottle of Southern Comfort (or your favorite bourbon)
6 oz of lemon juice
1 6 oz can of frozen lemonade
1 6 oz can of frozen orange juice
3 liters of lemon-lime soda
1 block of ice
2 lemons
2 oranges

We like this drink because you can make a big batch and it is self serve! Mix the first 4 ingredients in a punch bowl. Add soda. Gently place block of ice into the punch bowl. Add sliced lemons and oranges for garnish.

Southern "Hurricane" Drink

Assorted "Southern" Beers.

Bloody Mary
1 1/2 oz vodka
3 oz tomato juice
1 dash of lemon juice
1/2 tsp worcestershire sauce
2-3 drops of tabasco sauce
salt
pepper
fresh celery or pickled string beans

Shake first 5 ingredients with crushed ice in a martini shaker. Fill an old fashioned glass with ice cubes. Strain drink into glass. Add salt and pepper to taste. Garnish with a stalk of celery or pickled string bean.

Assorted Beers
You can find different types of beer at specialty stores, like Trader Joes. We found a Dixie brand. Always have a few familiar labels and enhance the options with a few specialty beers that compliment your theme.

Lemonade with Strawberries
You can purchase sweetened or unsweetend frozen strawberries. We preferred the unsweetend as it didn't cut the tartness of the lemonade. However, the sweetend tasted good too. If you will be having lots of children at your party, you may want to double this recipe.

2 cans frozen lemonade
1-16 oz package of frozen strawberries (sweetened or unsweetened)
Water

Make this in two batches so that it fits into your blender. In a blender mix 1 can of lemonade, 8 oz of strawberries and a can of water. Once blended, pour into a large pitcher and add additional water per instructions on lemonade can. Add ice to the pitcher and serve.

Assorted Non-Alcoholic Beverages
soda, diet, regular and caffeine free
bottled water

The Grocery List - Casual Cajun

Two weeks before the party

- ❒ 1 box Zatarain's crab boil
- ❒ 2 boxes Zatarain's dirty rice
- ❒ 1 bottle of hot pepper sauce, like Tabasco
- ❒ Sesame oil
- ❒ Olive oil
- ❒ Sugar
- ❒ Honey
- ❒ 1 bottle lemon juice
- ❒ Season salt
- ❒ Cayenne pepper
- ❒ Vanilla bean
- ❒ 1 bottle worcestershire sauce
- ❒ Vegtable oil
- ❒ 1 small bottle of mayonnaise
- ❒ 1 bottle rice vinegar
- ❒ 1 bottle vinegar
- ❒ 1 bottle white balsamic vinegar
- ❒ 1 bottle tomato juice
- ❒ 1 can syrup (cane, fruit or maple)
- ❒ 1 bottle of Southern Comfort
- ❒ 1 bottle Irish Whisky
- ❒ 1 bottle vodka
- ❒ Assorted Dixie beers
- ❒ 2 cans frozen lemonade
- ❒ 1 box or bag of frozen strawberries
- ❒ Soda, diet, regalar, caffiene free
- ❒ Bottled water
- ❒ Candles
- ❒ Matches
- ❒ 1 box large Ziplock baggies

Day before the party

- ❒ 16 oz 1/2 and 1/2
- ❒ 1 pint whole milk
- ❒ 2 c heavy cream (whipping)
- ❒ 1 c sour cream
- ❒ 1 8 oz cream cheese
- ❒ 2 lbs shrimp
- ❒ 2 lbs assorted Louisiana hot links
- ❒ 2 lbs ground chicken
- ❒ 2 lemons
- ❒ 12 artichokes
- ❒ 1 lb butter
- ❒ 1 dozen large eggs
- ❒ 1 container of Cool Whip or can of whipped cream
- ❒ 1 clove garlic
- ❒ 1 red bell pepper
- ❒ 1 green bell pepper
- ❒ 2 ripe mangos
- ❒ 6 shallots
- ❒ 2 Anahiem chilies
- ❒ 4 jalapenos
- ❒ 2 pound cakes
- ❒ 2 baskets strawberries
- ❒ 2 baskets raspberries
- ❒ 2 baskets blackberries
- ❒ 1 basket blueberries

Assorted prepared appetizers
- ❒ Jalapeno poppers
- ❒ Olive Tepenade
- ❒ Assorted artesian breads (sourdough, olive etc.)

The Time Line - Casual Cajun

Four weeks before the party
- ☐ Determine budget
- ☐ Identify location, determine date/time/ ambiance
- ☐ Compile guest list
- ☐ Purchase invitations if necessary
- ☐ Address and mail invitations

Two weeks before party
- ☐ Assess party set up needs: linens/serving pieces/dinnerware etc. (get everything out, wash what needs to be cleaned, polish silver if necessary etc.
- ☐ Place rental order if needed (chairs/ dinnerware) or call family to borrow pieces
- ☐ Main grocery shopping (see shopping list)

One week before party
- ☐ Pick up serving pieces (plastic/borrowed)
- ☐ Thoroughly clean house (see home preparation section)

One day before party
- ☐ Purchase perishables (see "last minute" grocery list)
- ☐ Make the lemonade
- ☐ Make the Mango relish
- ☐ Dice red and green peppers; store in sealed baggy; refrigerate;
- ☐ Brown ground chicken; store in tupperware; refrigerate
- ☐ Set table with linens and decor (not perishables), set out serving pieces and utensils (if an indoor party)

The day of the party one - two hours prior
- ☐ Assemble the bread pudding and refrigerate, don't bake. Make cream and caramel sauces
- ☐ Prep fruit for pound cake dessert; slice and platter pound cake, cover tightly with plastic wrap
- ☐ Make open house punch
- ☐ Ice the beer, soda, and bottled water in a large tub or ice chest
- ☐ Set up bar to make individual drinks if you are planning to do so
- ☐ Make dirty rice
- ☐ Steam and Broil artichokes
- ☐ Heat appetizers; platter cold ones
- ☐ During final dinner preparation, remove bread pudding from refrigerator and bring to room temperature. While guests are dining, bake bread pudding.

From top center: Shrimp Cocktail, Crab & Pea Celery Boats, Artichoke Dip with Assorted Crackers, California Rolls, Latkes, Asparagus Crepes, Mushroom Turnovers and Spinach Balls with Mustard Sauce.

The Classy Cocktail Buffet

This party is a lot of fun, but can be time consuming. Be careful with selecting too many hot appetizers as they require attention during the party. You may find that this party warrants the hiring of some teen assistants to keep hot appetizers warm and refreshed. We give you lots of choices with this menu. We suggest for a party of 20 that you limit the number of hot appetizers to four, not including the hot dips. Be sure to follow the time line so you don't end up in the kitchen when your guests are arriving!

Our friends and family really enjoyed this party. The variety of the appetizers, with differing textures, tastes and ingredients were really appreciated. The HIT of this party was the chocolate fondue. Make sure you have lots of plates and forks for dipping!

This is a great party for inside or out, so don't let weather hold you back...serve a martini, munch on a crab cake and enjoy your friends.

One special note. Cocktail parties are usually a scheduled event, with a beginning and an end time. 5:00 to 8:00 pm is the usual time. Our friends, however, stayed late and ate EVERYTHING!! If this happens to you, you may want to order pizza or something else to be delivered to feed the partiers. When serving alcohol, you need to make sure people have plenty to eat and an assortment of nonalcoholic beverages such as bottled water, soda, and coffee. And make sure everyone has a safe ride home.

What You Need For This Party:

Serving Pieces needed for this Party:
3 small glass or crystal bowls
1 glass pedestal or standard bowl
7 round, oval or rectangular platters
1 large basket w/ a pretty napkin to line
2 casserole dishes
1 raised cake plate
1 fondue pot with 20 long forks
20 lunch-size plates
20 forks
12 wine glasses
15 Martini glasses
12 coffee cups
40 napkins
large Martini Shaker
large tub or ice chest for beer

Cooking Utensils needed for this Party:
large mixing bowl
medium mixing bowl
cookie sheets
small sauce pan
small frying pan
medium frying pan
steamer
cutting board
knives (serrated, chef and paring)
cheese grater
measuring spoons, cups and glass measurer
slotted spoon
wax paper
paper towels
coffee pot

Mushroom Turnovers and Spinach Balls with Mustard Sauce

Spinach Balls with Mustard Sauce

Number of Servings	12
Serving Dishes	Platter or raised cake plate
Preparation Time	20 minutes
Cooking Time	10-15 minutes
Can You Double	No
Can You Freeze	No

Spinach Balls

2 10 oz pkgs frozen chopped spinach, thawed and squeezed dry.
2 c of herb stuffing mix, crushed
1 c firmly packed grated Parmesan cheese (use only fresh whole and grate or freshly grated)
1/2 c (1 stick) butter, melted
4 sm green onions, finely chopped
3 eggs
Dash of nutmeg

Preheat oven to 350 degrees. Combine all ingredients in a large bowl and mix well. Shape into 1 inch balls. Cover and refrigerate (or freeze) until ready to bake. Set balls on an ungreased baking sheet and bake until golden brown and a little crispy on the edges, approximately 10 to 15 minutes. Serve with Mustard Sauce.

Mustard Sauce

1/2 c dry mustard
1/2 c white vinegar
1/4 c sugar
1 egg yolk

Combine mustard and vinegar in a small bowl. Cover and let stand at room temperate for 4 hours. Mix sugar and egg yolk in a small saucepan. Add mustard/vinegar mixture and cook over low heat, stirring continually until slightly thickened. Cover and chill. Serve at room temperature.

Asparagus Crepes

Asparagus Crepes

Number of Servings	12
Serving Dishes	Platter or raised cake plate
Preparation Time	20 minutes
Cooking Time	None
Can You Double	No
Can You Freeze	No

Crepe
1/2 c all purpose flour
1/2 c milk
1/4 c lukewarm water
2 large eggs
2 T unsalted butter, melted
1/2 tsp salt
additional butter for cooking the crepes

Combine ingredients in a blender or food processor until smooth. Pour the batter into a bowl. Cover with plastic wrap and let stand for 30 minutes (or you can refrigerate up to two days). Place a nonstick pan (small frying pan works fine) over medium heat. Coat the pan with a little butter (about a teaspoon). Stir the batter and pour about a tablespoon into the pan, lifting the pan off of the heat and rotating it so that the batter forms an even, fine layer. Cook until the top is set and the underside golden. Turn the crepes over, using a spatula or your fingers and cook until the second side is lightly browned. Remove the crepe and place on a piece of parchment paper. Use a drinking glass or biscuit cutter that is about 3-4 inches in diameter to cut the crepe into a smooth round shape. Continue cooking the remainder of the crepes, stirring the batter and adding butter to the pan each time you start a new crepe. Stack, cut, finished crepes between parchment paper. Use immediately, or let cool, wrap air tight in foil and plastic wrap, and freeze for up to one month, or refrigerate if using the next day. Let crepes come to room temperature before filling. This recipe makes approximately 2 dozen 4 inch crepes.

Filling
1/2 lb fresh asparagus or 1 (9 oz) pkg of frozen (use fresh if you can as it yields a better texture)
1 5 oz pkg of herbed cream cheese, at room temperature

Cook asparagus in a small amount of boiling, salted water until crisp tender; about 3 minutes (watch closely by piercing it with a fork while cooking or asparagus will over cook and be mushy). Cut off end of spear so that each spear is about 1/2 inch longer than the diameter of the crepes. Spread each crepe with the cream cheese, placing the asparagus tip in the center and roll up. Serve at room temperature or cold.

Crab & Pea Celery Boats.

Crab & Pea Celery Boats

Number of Servings	12-15 (makes 5 dozen)
Serving Dishes	Platter
Preparation Time	20 minutes (filling can be made the night before and assembled the day of the party
Cooking Time	None
Can You Double	Yes
Can You Freeze	No

8-10 wide celery ribs, trimmed
¼ c cream cheese (2 oz), softened
2 T mayonnaise
1 T plus 1 tsp of Fresh lemon juice
1 T finely chopped basil
2 tsp finely chopped tarragon
2 tsp finely chopped flat-leaf parsley
½ tsp finely grated lemon zest
½ lb lump crab meat, picked over and well drained
½ c frozen baby peas, thawed
½ c finely chopped fennel bulb, plus fennel fronds (for garnish, if desired)
3 T finely chopped red onion
kosher salt and freshly ground pepper

Cut a thin slice off the back of the celery ribs so they will sit flat on your serving dish and cut them on the diagonal into 1-inch lengths.

In a medium bowl, combine the softened cream cheese with the mayonnaise, lemon juice, basil, tarragon, parsley and lemon zest. Add the crab meat, peas, fennel bulb and onion and stir gently until just combined. Season with kosher salt and pepper. Spoon about a tablespoon of the crab salad onto each piece of celery and garnish with a bit of fennel frond.

Make Ahead: The crab salad can be refrigerated for up to 1 day.   The celery ribs can also be cut and readied a day ahead (place in ice water and refrigerate) and assembled the day of the party. Another way to serve this salad is to spoon it onto challah toasts.

California Rolls

Assorted Purchased Appetizers

Number of Servings	12
Serving Dishes	Platter or raised cake plate
Preparation Time	20 minutes
Cooking Time	None
Can You Double	No
Can You Freeze	No

You can find numerous pre-made appetizers in the frozen and deli sections of your grocery store. Specialty grocery stores, like Trader Joes, offer quite a selection. We suggest you pick three out of the following (or pick your favorites from your local store):

- Latkes (frozen); appetizer size. Cook as directed on the package.
- Mini Quiches (frozen); small, bite size, not the large entre portion. Cook as directed on the package.
- Bruchetta (cold case, found in the deli) serve with toasted french or sourdough baguette, sliced
- Shrimp Cocktail with Sauce (frozen, precooked shrimp) we recommend defrosting in the refrigerator.
- California Rolls - Sushi with Soy Sauce (fresh from the cold case). This must be REALLY fresh!

Crab Souffle Dip

Number of Servings	12
Serving Dishes	Small casserole and platter
Preparation Time	15 minutes
Cooking Time	40 minutes
Can You Double	No
Can You Freeze	No

8 oz softened cream cheese
3/4 c mayonnaise
1 beaten egg
1 T grated onion or shallot
2 tsp lemon juice

8 oz crab meat
1 tsp parsley
1/4 c grated parmesan cheese
2 T butter
Assorted sturdy crackers.

Pre-heat oven to 350 degrees. In a medium size mixing bowl, mix together the cream cheese and mayonnaise. Add the egg, onion, lemon juice, crab meat, parsley and parmesan cheese. Grease a casserole dish with butter. Pour crab mixture into the prepared casserole dish. Bake for 35-45 minutes - until golden brown. Can be served warm or at room temperature. When ready to serve, place casserole on platter and surround with assorted crackers.

Crudites with Assorted Dips

Number of Servings	12
Serving Dishes	Platter or raised cake plate
Preparation Time	20 minutes
Cooking Time	None
Can You Double	No
Can You Freeze	No

2 pkgs baby carrots or cut carrots
2 pkgs of cut celery
1 head/pkg of cauliflower
1 head/pkg of broccoli

1 basket of cherry tomatoes
4 small zucchini (cut to size of celery)
4 crooked neck yellow squash (cut to size of celery)
1 bunch radishes, cleaned with ends cut off

For the Dip
Prepared dips found in the cold case deli or make package dips such as ranch and vegetable. If using a dry package mix, you will likely need the following: 1 pkg dry di, 1 c sour cream and 1 c mayonnaise

Stuffed Mushrooms

Number of Servings	12
Serving Dishes	Platter or raised cake plate
Preparation Time	20 minutes
Cooking Time	7 to 10 minutes
Can You Double	Yes
Can You Freeze	No

2 pkgs (8 oz each) cream cheese, softened
1 onion, finely chopped
6 slices of bacon, cooked, drained and crumbled
18 medium white mushrooms, cleaned and dried
1/4 c grated fresh parmesan cheese

Turn on broiler. Brown bacon, remove from pan and drain on paper towels. Brown onions in bacon fat. Drain onions on a paper towel. Mix bacon, onions and cream cheese. Clean mushrooms and remove stems. Fill mushrooms with cream cheese mixture and sprinkle with parmesan cheese. Broil until cheese is slightly browned. (Watch carefully so they don't burn!)

Artichoke Dip with Assorted Crackers

Number of Servings	12
Serving Dishes	Ovenproof casserole dish and basket
Preparation Time	20 minutes
Cooking Time	20-25 minutes
Can You Double	No
Can You Freeze	No

2 jars (6 oz each) marinated artichoke hearts, chopped
1 pkg (10 oz) frozen chopped spinach, thawed and drained
1/2 tsp chopped garlic or 1 garlic clove, chopped
1/2 c sour cream

1/2 c mayonnaise
3/4 c grated parmesan cheese
Assorted crackers

Preheat oven to 375. Drain and coarsely chop artichoke hearts. In a medium bowl mix all remaining ingredients. Pour into a medium casserole dish. Bake 20 - 25 minutes, until heated through and bubbly. Serve with sturdy crackers.

Chocolate Fondue

Number of Servings	20
Serving Dishes	Fondue pan with forks, large platter
Preparation Time	20 minutes
Cooking Time	10 minutes
Can You Double	Yes
Can You Freeze	Yes, up to 6 months (chocolate sauce only)

1 pint (2 c) heavy cream
10 oz best-quality bittersweet or semisweet chocolate, like Lindt, cut into small pieces
Fresh strawberries, bananas, kiwi, pears, pineapple, tangerines, dried apricots, marshmallows, pound cake

Melt chocolate in a double boiler or in a sauce pan over low heat. Stir continually to avoid burning. Once melted, remove from heat. Pour cream into a 1 1/2 quart saucepan set over medium heat. When the cream begins to simmer, lower the heat and add the melted chocolate. Whisk for 1 minute over low heat, then turn off the heat. Continue whisking until the mixture is smooth. Cool slightly before using. The sauce will remain liquid at room temperature for about 2 hours, then it will thicken. You can soften it by reheating it on low over the stove top and whisking until heated through.

Note: Because fruit is seasonal, we have provided a variety of items to dip. Clean and peel fruit, except the pears. Platter in groups of like items. Use regular forks if you don't have enough fondue forks.

Notes

Pitchers and Glasses of Martini's; Sour Apple, Lemon Drop and Classic Cosmopolitan.

Martini

The Classy Cocktails & Beverages

Sour Apple Martini
2 parts Sour Apple Pucker
2 parts Vodka (Ketel One recommended)
1 part Triple Sec
Thinly sliced granny smith apple or Maraschino cherry for garnish

Fill martini shaker with crushed ice. Measure in liquid ingredients. Close lid and shake until martini shaker is frosted and cold. Pour into martini glasses and garnish. This martini is sweet.

Lemon Drop Martini
2 parts Absolut Citron
1 part Triple Sec
1 part Lime Juice
Lemon rind for garnish

Fill martini shaker with crushed ice. Measure in liquid ingredients. Close lid and shake until martini shaker is frosted and cold. Pour into martini glasses and garnish. This martini is tart.

Classic Cosmopolitan Martini
1 part Vodka (Ketel One or SKYY recommended; if making Sour Apple, use the same brand for both)
2 parts Cranberry Juice
1 part Roses Lime Cordial
1 part Triple Sec
Lemon rind for garnish

Fill martini shaker with crushed ice. Measure in liquid ingredients. Close lid and shake until martini shaker is frosted and cold. Pour into martini glasses and garnish.

Assorted Beers
Heiniken, Samual Adams, Miller Genuine Draft - include your favorite!

Assorted nonalcoholic Drinks
Cola, diet cola, 7-up/sprite, bottled water, etc.

The Grocery List - Classy Cocktail

Two weeks before the party

- ☐ 1 box herb stuffing mix
- ☐ 20 oz parmesean cheese; grated
- ☐ 2 sticks of butter
- ☐ 1 doz large eggs
- ☐ Nutmeg
- ☐ 4 oz dry mustard
- ☐ 1 sm bottle of white vinegar
- ☐ Sugar
- ☐ 1 large jar of mayonnaise
- ☐ 1 bottle of lemon juice
- ☐ 1 bottle of lime juice*
- ☐ 2 jars of cocktail sauce**
- ☐ Soy sauce**
- ☐ 4 boxes of assorted sturdy crackers
- ☐ 2 6 oz jars of marinated artichoke hearts
- ☐ 1 sm jar of chopped garlic
- ☐ 3 10 oz package frozen spinach
- ☐ 1 package frozen peas

Assorted frozen appetizers
- ☐ 3 pkg crab cakes
- ☐ 2 pkg latkes
- ☐ 2 boxes mini quiches
- ☐ 2 pkg cooked, deveined, peeled, tail on shrimp
- ☐ Assorted beers; Heiniken, Samual Adams, MGD
- ☐ Cola, Diet cola, 7-up/sprite, bottled water
- ☐ Vodka (Ketel One or SKYY recommended) *
- ☐ Triple Sec*
- ☐ Apple Pucker*
- ☐ Absolute Citron Vodka*
- ☐ Roses Lime Cordial*
- ☐ Cranberry juice*
- ☐ Candles
- ☐ Matches

Day before the party

- ☐ 1 bunch green onions
- ☐ 1/2 lb fresh asparagus
- ☐ 2 packages of baby carrots or cut carrots
- ☐ 3 bundles of celery stalks
- ☐ 1 head cauliflower
- ☐ 1 large head broccoli
- ☐ 1 basket cherry tomatoes
- ☐ 4 medium zucchini
- ☐ 4 medium yellow squash
- ☐ 1 bunch radishes
- ☐ 1 fennel bulb
- ☐ 1 red onion
- ☐ 1 white or yellow onion
- ☐ 18 medium mushrooms
- ☐ 2 lemons
- ☐ 1 bunch flat leaf parsley
- ☐ 1 bunch fresh tarragon
- ☐ 1 bunch fresh basil
- ☐ 5 oz herbed cream cheese
- ☐ 4 8 oz packages cream cheese
- ☐ 1 package bacon
- ☐ Kosher salt
- ☐ Black Pepper
- ☐ 2 packages california rolls (sushi)**
- ☐ Sourdough baguette**
- ☐ Bruchetta**
- ☐ Prepared Dip or
  - ☐ Dry packaged dip***
  - ☐ Sour cream***
- ☐ 10 oz Lindt or best quality bitter or semi-sweet chocolate
- ☐ 1 pint heavy cream
- ☐ Assorted fruit, pound cake, marshmallows etc.

* Purchase if you are going to make the martini's. If you are only going to offer one kind, cross out the ingredients for the others you are not going to make.

** Purchase only if you purchase the frozen appetizers that complement the condiments.

The Time Line - Classy Cocktail

Four weeks before the party
- [ ] Determine budget
- [ ] Identify location; determine the date, time, ambiance
- [ ] Compile guest list
- [ ] Order more invitations if necessary
- [ ] Address and mail invitations

Two weeks before party
- [ ] Assess party set up needs: linens/serving pieces/ dinnerware etc. (get everything out, wash what needs to be cleaned, polish silver if necessary etc. This can be very time consuming so don't delay. You will also find that if you need to rent or borrow something, you will have adequate time to do so.
- [ ] Place rental order if needed (chairs/dinnerware) or call family to borrow pieces
- [ ] Main grocery shopping (see shopping list)
- [ ] Make spinach balls to the point of forming into balls. Place them on a cookie sheet and freeze for 30 minutes. romove the balls from the cookie sheet and wrap in foil and then plastic wrap. Freeze.
- [ ] Make the crepes, placing them on parchment paper as they are cooked, layering parchment, crepe, parch ment, crepe until you have run out of batter. Place parchment over the last crepe. Wrap in foil and plastic wrap. Freeze.

One week before party
- [ ] Pick up serving pieces (plastic/borrowed)
- [ ] If hosting the party outside: Mow the lawns, weed, spruce up potted plants by removing struggling plants and adding fresh, vibrant plants. Plant brightly colored plants in pots for the centerpieces of your tables (baby roses or gerber daisies are nice) and the serving table, wash down the patio area.
- [ ] Thorough house cleaning (see home preparation section)

One day before party
- [ ] Purchase perishables (see "last minute" grocery list)
- [ ] Remove shrimp, spinach balls and crepes from the freezer, defrost in the refrigerator.
- [ ] Make crab and pea filling.
- [ ] Make dip for crudites platter
- [ ] Wash and cut vegetables, place in bowls with ice water, refrigerate. (Be sure to keep the broccoli in a separate bowl.
- [ ] Make artichoke dip to the point of baking, do not bake, refrigerate
- [ ] Clean mushrooms, remove stems and dry VERY well; refrigerate
- [ ] Make stuffed mushroom filling, refrigerate
- [ ] Set table with linens and decor (not perishables), set out serving pieces and utensils (if an indoor party)

The day of the party
- [ ] Remove crab and pea filling from refrigerator; let stand 15 - 20 minutes to soften; then fill celery per recipe.
- [ ] Remove mushroom filling, mushrooms, spinach balls and crepes from the refrigerator and let them come to room temperature; about 30 minutes.
- [ ] Make the crab souffle
- [ ] Bake spinach balls per recipe
- [ ] Platter the shrimp and place cocktail sauce in a serving bowl
- [ ] Assemble the aspargus crepes
- [ ] Take artichoke dip out of the refrigerator and sit out on counter until room temperature; bake per recipe
- [ ] Platter vegetables and place dip in a serving bowl
- [ ] Fill mushrooms with filling and broil per recipe
- [ ] Bake assorted frozen appetizers
- [ ] Setup up bar

House Preparation for Guests and Clean Up

Your home is already filled with decorations that represent your personal style. Decorating, therefore, is really limited to small touches that will add elegance and warmth. However, your house should be very clean and tidy, which depending on how much of a collector you are, may take more time than you think to clean up. Below are guidelines for getting your home ready for your guests.

1. Do a thorough cleaning of your home a week prior to your party. Scrub down all rooms that will be inhabited by your guests. Note, if some guests have not been to your home they will likely be asking for a tour. You will need to clean up all the rooms. Dust, vacuum, swipe cob webs, clean windows that are easily seen, wipe down all shelves and knickknacks. Clean the oven, stove, and refrigerator (throw out those science projects). Mop all the floors, clean mirrors etc. Throw out or store out of sight old newspapers, magazines and junk mail.

2. The day before, do a walk-through of your home and touch up rooms that need sprucing. The bathroom usually requires a quick wipe down, and the vacuum may need to be run over the carpets. Wipe down the kitchen after you have finished the majority of your food preparation, otherwise you just have to clean up again!

3. Make sure you have laundered fresh towels for the bathroom and kitchen. It is nice to have finger tip towels on the counter in the bathroom for guests to use. A basket of washcloths is also a nice touch. Put out extra rolls of toilet paper in a basket near the toilet, that way guests can help themselves if necessary. Scented soaps are also appreciated, as are lotion and tissue.

4. Many times the plan of a party and friends coming over sparks the idea for a home project, like painting the kitchen or building a deck! Trust us, we know. The good part is that you get things done you have been wanting to do, but hadn't found the time. The problem is that the projects are usually more time consuming than one thinks and the project ends up usurping time that should be spent on party preparation. Think carefully over what added projects the party may inspire. If you have a significant other who is gung ho, just make sure they understand the time limitations and that you will be busy with the party preparations.

5. Clean up is an important aspect of a party. For one, you do not have your guests wash dishes. They came to your home to visit and be away from household chores. If they politely offer, politely refuse. Stack dishes neatly in your kitchen, we always try to rinse the dishes and stack them that way they are easier to clean later. You will need to put perishable food away. Make sure you have plastic wrap, foil and storage containers for leftovers.

6. Throw out dairy products and seafood that has been sitting out many hours. Do not pour cream or milk back into the original container, as you will spoil the unused portion. If you just put out a new pitcher of cream and feel it is still cold, cover the pitcher tightly with plastic wrap and refrigerate.

Helpful Hints

1. Have trash receptacles available and easily accessible, guests will use them if they can find them.
2. Wear an apron over your clothing while baking and have a beautiful fresh one just for the day of the party for setting out food this will protect your party clothes.
3. If you feel like you need help, you can hire servers to assist you with set up, serving and clean up. Hourly rate for professionals are $15 - $20 per hour plus tip. For a lower rate, obtain the assistance from responsible teenagers looking for extra income.
4. Create drink area as self serve, this way you only have to worry about making another large pot of coffee and not pouring individual cups.
5. If you can afford it, have your house cleaned. This will save you lots of time and lots of energy. If not, clean it well the weekend before, with touch up the evening before or morning of the party.
6. Have a secure place designated for coats and purses.
7. Anything with a cream/milk ingredient needs to be monitored for coolness. If you have an item that will be out for many hours, like the cream for the coffee, the pitcher should be placed in a bowl of ice.
8. You do, however, need to watch for empty plates and used napkins and remove them as you roam the party, to keep the location of your party in fairly nice shape. Once the buffet is pretty well emptied and your guests are mulling around in another room enjoying their beverage and conversation, you can quickly wrap up and put away the remaining food, but don't start doing dishes. Turn out the light of your kitchen and buffet area, and go enjoy your guests.
9. Specify if children are invited. Evening, formal parties are not really appropriate. Children get bored.
10. Find out if any of your guests have special dietary needs. If so, be sure to have appropriate beverage and food items.
11. If you are having children, review the menu you have selected. You may need to add a few kid-friendly dishes from your local store. Be sure to add these items to your grocery list.
12. If you live in an area with limited parking, you may need to hire a valet service. You will need to check with City Hall for any required permits.
13. If you have rented linens, serving pieces, tables or chairs, be sure to call and order early, especially around a holiday, otherwise color choices and selection may be limited.
14. If your party is outdoors, and your sprinkler system is automatic, be sure to turn them off the day prior to your party to avoid muddy areas or worse, your sprinkler system activating in the middle of your party.
15. If you have young guests, be sure to have games or other activities planned to entertain them.
16. Also make sure your house is "child proof" this will save both you and the parents heartache.
17. The parties were designed for 20 guests. If you have less, alter your menu accordingly. If you have more, use a favorite recipe or ask a friend to bring an item. Just remember to make adjustments to the grocery lists and timelines.

Notes

Recipe Index